Soaring with Eagles

Soaring with Eagles

❧

The Life and Legacy of Frank J. Blau Jr.

Ellen Rohr and Helena Bouchez

Published In Partnership With Nexstar Network, Inc.

Nexstar Network
101 E. Fifth Street. Suite 2100
Saint Paul, MN 55101

Book Layout ©2013 BookDesignTemplates.com
Book Title/ Author Name. —1st ed.
ISBN: 153038088X
ISBN13: 9781530380886
CreateSpace Independent Publishing Platform
North Charleston, South Carolina

Contents

Leaders are like eagles.
They are rare. They don't flock.
You find them one at a time.
They see life from a higher vantage point.

To all Frank's eagles.

If you learn anything in this world that is valuable, you must share it with your fellow man before you die because each generation must have it better than the previous generation.

— MARIE BLAU

CHAPTER 1

—⸙—

Early Life

FRANK J. BLAU Jr. arrived on planet Earth on February 23, 1929, at the height of the Roaring Twenties, exactly eight months ahead of the Wall Street stock market crash that would launch the United States into the Great Depression.

He was the firstborn son of Polish immigrants Frank J. and Marie Blau and the grandson of Rosalee and John Crason. Three siblings would follow: Jimmy, Margie, and then Eddie, the baby of the family.

In 1930[1], the elder Frank was working for a plumbing supply house, and the family lived on Fratney Street, close to the Milwaukee River, in Milwaukee, Wisconsin. Even so, the Depression hit the Blau family hard. "We didn't have *anything*," says Frank Jr.

Young Entrepreneur

Before he was ten, Frank Jr. understood that if he wanted something, it was up to him to figure out how to earn the money needed to get it. And so he set his mind to it.

Frank recalls an early lesson on how to earn money.

There was a government relief station where you could pick up rations, but it was more than a mile away, and many of our neighbors were elderly and couldn't make it there. I used to go around and collect ration stamps from people in the neighborhood and travel to the relief center with an empty coaster wagon and fill it with goodies, brown bags packed with split peas and other food.

The wagon was light on the way there, but once it was loaded up, it was really heavy and a pretty hard tow for a little kid. These folks trusted me, little Frankie Blau, just nine years old, to pick up their stuff. When I got back, I would distribute the materials and food to the neighbors, and they'd give me pennies.

Frank Jr. saw other opportunities to earn money and was quick to act.

"We lived in the Polish area of Milwaukee," he says, "and every street corner had a tavern. There was no bottled or canned beer then; it was all strictly draft at the counter. Men would come in and drink draft beer; some would bring a bucket to fill with beer to carry back to home. I used to catch crayfish at the river near where we lived and sell them at the taverns."

In the process, Frank noticed many shoes that could use a shine. "So, I built a shoe shine box. On Fridays I would go into the taverns and say to the men sitting at the bar, 'Shoe shine, mister?' I charged five cents a shoe. I'd be down on my knees, shining away, while they sat on bar stools with their feet on the shoe shine box."

Shining shoes was lucrative, but it wasn't glamorous. "In those parts, a lot of the men chewed tobacco, and so there were a number of spittoons on the floor," Frank says. "When guys spat, they were very accurate, but when the tobacco juice landed, the juice would splash up on me—and onto my glasses. I had to always carry a damp towel with me to clean them off."

So young Frank fetched and delivered rations to his neighbors, sold crayfish he'd caught in the Milwaukee River, and shined shoes at the taverns. He also set up a Kool-Aid stand and collected discarded bus passes; he resold those with a little left over.

Frank says he developed an entrepreneurial spirit, because his family didn't have anything. Not having anything motivated Frank to work very hard to earn money so he could have something. This willingness to work hard to create a better life stayed with Frank for the rest of his life.

Frank's childhood wasn't all work and no play, however. "I'd save a little money but also spend a little on a pineapple marshmallow sundae—or a soda and a hamburger," Frank recalls.

Competitive Spirit

In between his various entrepreneurial pursuits, Frank attended a Catholic grade school and participated in sports through the Catholic Youth Organization (CYO) programs. Frank liked sports, but he loved to compete. He and his CYO buddies dreamed of becoming high school sports stars. The school they dreamed of attending was Messmer High School, a private school the local Catholic diocese ran.

The problem was, Frank's father, a salesman for a wholesale plumbing supplies house, wanted Frank to become a plumber. He tried to steer Frank toward the public vocational school, which offered a plumbing program that would enable Frank to knock off three years of the five-year plumbing apprenticeship while he was still in high school.

Working as a plumbing materials salesman, Frank's father assumed that plumbers made a lot of money. Plus, the vocational school was a public school, so there would be no tuition. "My father said, 'If you want to go to a private school, they charge tuition. I'm not going to pay for it.'" Frank Jr. responded, "I'll pay my own way." Not to be deterred, Frank enrolled at Messmer and paid his own tuition by working part-time in a filling station, pumping gas and cleaning up the place.

Participating in high school athletics reinforced Frank's desire to compete, to be the best at whatever he did and to win. As a senior, Frank was among an elite group of football players from five different schools named to the Milwaukee Catholic High School all-star team.

FRANK BLAU— – Senior. Two years on squad. Also plays hockey, basketball, boxes. 5″, 8 1/2″″, 145 lbs. Three letterman.

The team traveled from Milwaukee to Minneapolis-St. Paul to take on the Twin City CYC Catholic high school all-stars—to win the state title.

"Winning that football title instilled within me the importance of building a winning team and was my proudest moment as an athlete," recalls Frank.

A "lettered" athlete, Frank also played hockey, basketball and was a member of the boxing team.

Get It in Writing

To keep his team in shape over the summer, the football coach obtained jobs for the players with a local potato farmer. Frank and his friend Zeke stayed on the guy's farm and worked long and hard during the day. At the end of the summer, the farmer paid Zeke and took both boys to the Greyhound station. They were to board a bus and go back home to Milwaukee.

"When we got on Greyhound bus," Frank says, "Zeke took out the money the farmer had given him and handed me half of it—$20. I found out the farmer had paid Zeke $40, instead of the *$400* we'd agreed to at the beginning of summer. I said, 'We worked our butts off all summer for $20 apiece!' I learned then and there to define the work and payment *in writing before* I did anything."

Fighting for Irene

During his freshman year, Frank met a girl in art class; her name was Irene Shimmels.

In addition to being a football star and hockey player, Frank was also a boxer—147-pound weight class. So when classmate and fellow boxer Paul Kruezer made a play for Irene, Frank warned him off. He said, "Lay off! She is my girl. If you and I ever make it to the ring together, I am going to crush you."

When they finally did get in the ring at a boxing tournament, sponsored by the high school's men's club, Frank nailed him in the first round and knocked him out in the third—in front of a crowd of eighteen hundred people, according to an article in the local newspaper.

Frank's boxing experience also taught him several valuable life lessons.

1. Prepare yourself mentally for oncoming tests and competition. Preparation includes having a plan of action.
2. Being physically fit ensures you can go the distance.
3. If your initial plan of action fails, you better know what plan B is.
4. When the going gets tough, the tough get going—even more so.
5. Having a good coach and mentor is critical to reaching success.
6. If we rely only on our own knowledge of how to succeed in life, we'll die impoverished and stupid.

Frank courted Irene throughout high school, taking her to their junior and senior proms. In spring 1947, Frank graduated from high school and headed off to college.

CHAPTER 2

Searching for the Future

IN FALL 1947, Frank enrolled in the Northern Illinois College of Optometry. He intended to become an optometrist, but soon he became homesick. Back in Milwaukee, Frank decided to become an undertaker. He changed his mind about that, however, after a number of people died on him in rapid succession (one literally).

Frank recalls, "The first time, I was in college. Mortuary science was my major. I was working a part-time job driving a truck. As I was driving, a body crashed onto the windshield. Suicide. The guy had jumped from the bridge above." He'd nearly taken Frank with him.

Three weeks later, Frank saw a train hit a car and bore witness to the grisly aftermath. That was number two.

The third time, just a few weeks after the train incident, Frank says, "I was driving with my dad and my brother on a country road, and we were passed by a car, going like hell. Then we saw shoes on the road. The car had hit a pedestrian crossing the highway on foot and knocked him out of his shoes. We were the first ones on the scene." Frank had seen enough, and that was the end of the mortuary science major.

A persistent Frank then enrolled in Marquette University, this time intending to become a dentist. The entrance exam included questions that tested his mechanical aptitude. Afraid of being pigeonholed as a mechanic, Frank purposely gave wrong answers and effectively weeded himself right out of the program.

Frank recalls, "I didn't think doctors and dentists were mechanics!"

Frank talked the department into letting him retake the exam, and this time he qualified. As it turned out, he probably would have made a fine dentist. But to get to dental school, he would first need to earn his degree in liberal arts.

Frank recalls, "I went to night school for a semester, but I had a love affair going on, and eventually I just decided it made more sense for me to go a different way."

Assembling Work

It was now 1949, and, needing to make some regular money, Frank got a second-shift job as an assembly line worker at the Seaman Auto Plant in Milwaukee.

At the time, Seaman manufactured car bodies for the Nash Car Company. They were then shipped fifteen miles south to a plant in Kenosha for assembly. "The Seaman plant eventually became part of American Motors Corporation," recalls Frank.

At Seaman, Frank became an expert spot welder and arc welder. He even considered pursuing welding as a career. The problem was the factory environment. From three o'clock in the afternoon until eleven o'clock in the evening, Frank felt imprisoned.

"I'd work second shift and go drink beer," he says. "I was courting Irene and trying to figure out 'What's next?'"

As oppressive as the job at the plant was, however, it paid $3.50 an hour. With overtime, that was more than double what most people made at the time. In 1948, median income was just $3,100 a year or about $1.49 per hour for full-time work.

Frank wanted to marry Irene and start a family. He also wanted to buy a house, so he decided to tough it out at the plant for a while longer. By the middle of 1950, however, the Korean War had broken out, and Frank became concerned that he would be drafted.

"So I called the induction center," Frank says. "I figured, what the hell? Before I get married and buy a house, I better find out if I'm going to be drafted. They said, 'Come down. We'll run you through a physical as if you've received a notice.' I passed everything—until they examined my eyeballs. The physician said, 'Are you kidding me? You can't see! We're looking for men who can kill.'"

Reassured by this response, Frank and Irene went forward with their plans. Based on his factory income, Frank bought a brand-new two-bedroom home with an attached garage and a washer and dryer for $11,000. It had a fireplace, which would provide an affordable way to heat the home, at least the living room. The mortgage was seventy-five dollars per month. "Everything a couple in 1950 could ever want," says Frank.

In October 1950, Frank and Irene were married. Six months later, Frank got a notice to appear at the induction center for a physical. He went through the process again—with the same results—and received a deferment. All was good.

A few months later, however, Frank got another notice, requiring him to appear for a physical *again*. Remembers Frank, "We'd based our decision to get married and start a family on the assumption I could not be drafted because of my eyesight, and now we had a house and a child on the way."

Shortly after that, Frank got a draft notice, marked "1A." It looked like Frank was going to be drafted after all. Frank recalls, "By that time we had *two* kids! I explained my situation to our family doctor, Dr. Ziegler, and he wrote me a letter, which led to deferment. Luckily, I wasn't ever drafted."

CHAPTER 3

Starting Over

THE PLANT CONTINUED to take its toll on Frank until the day he found out from his parents that his brother Jimmy had received a postcard from the local plumbers' union, stating he should come to their office and take the plumber aptitude test. The only problem was that Jimmy was now in the air force.

"When my parents told me about that, it got me thinking," says Frank.

For Frank, working at a factory was like being in prison with work release. And even though he had learned to weld at Seaman Auto Plant, inwardly Frank didn't feel that work was what he wanted to do for the rest of his life.

"So, I called plumbers' union and told them, 'This is Frank Blau. I want to take the place of my brother Jim and take the aptitude test.' They said that wasn't possible, that I would have to come in and sign an application to become a plumber, and they would advise me whether or not I could take the test. So, I did that, and then I forgot all about it."

A few months later, a notice from the plumbers' union arrived in Frank's mailbox, stating that he, Frank J. Blau Jr., should appear for an aptitude test. Thus, Frank and Irene began the process of carefully considering the impact this decision could have on their lives.

At $3.50 per hour, Frank brought in $540 a month in income; thus a $75 monthly mortgage was well within their means. An apprentice's initial pay rate, however, would be just $0.74 per hour—a whopping 70 percent pay cut. Frank would go from making $140 per week to just $118 per *month*, with only $43 per month left over after making the house payment.

Recalls Frank, "I talked to Irene, and together we thought very carefully about this move. It was a very serious what-if discussion. Irene was supportive. We both agreed that in the long haul, a career as a tradesman would prove more rewarding."

Frank's next step was to approach Ray Cook, the local banker who had the mortgage on their house. "When I told Ray what my plans were, he implored me not to do it. 'Don't do this!' he said. 'We'll end up owning your home.' I told Ray, 'You're not going to wind up getting my house, and I'm going to make you eat those words.'"

Frank took the test. All he and Irene could do now was wait and try to manage their anxiety over a future that was suddenly uncertain. Then, in early May 1951, the letter from the plumbers' union finally arrived. Frank had met the qualifications for the apprenticeship.

"I showed the letter to Irene. We read it and then sat in silence, looking into each other's eyes for what seemed to be forever, contemplating the ramifications of this fateful decision," recalls Frank.

Despite the prospect of going broke and the potential of losing everything, Frank and Irene's decision would stand. On June 10, 1951, he signed on as a plumber's apprentice and chucked the factory job for good. He was twenty-one years old.

Inching-Up Income

"The union training was a five-year program, and we would get a little raise every six months," recalls Frank.

As an apprentice, I should always have been working with another plumber who was licensed, but usually when that plumber realized I knew what I was doing, he'd leave me alone to do the work. Well, the owner eventually realized this and said, "Frank, did you do all this alone? Piss on the union rules. You deserve a raise," and he raised my pay—to ninety-nine cents per hour. Later, I asked him to give me a one-cent raise so I would be making one dollar per hour. Well, this led to a big altercation, and I ended up swinging a pipe wrench at the guy to protect myself. The guy eventually went out of business. Naturally, he became a plumbing inspector.

As Frank worked his way toward journeyman status, the kids kept coming: Joanie in '51, Jimmy in '52, and Frank E. in '54. Frank wanted to create a good life for his family. He wanted them to have something, so he worked hard and saved money, even adding a second job stocking shelves at Kohl's. "Finish plumbing…and off to Kohl's," recalls Frank. He also started taking on plumbing side jobs.

Butler Auto Body

In 1955, Frank achieved journeyman status as a plumber. It was an accomplishment, but Frank found it hard to celebrate. He had come to the conclusion that a journeyman's paycheck wasn't going to be enough to keep up with the needs of his growing family. He had three kids already, and a fourth (Tommy) was on the way.

About the same time, Frank's brother Jimmy returned from the service and started an auto body repair business—Butler Auto Body in Butler, Wisconsin. Jim asked Frank to join him as an owner. After assuring Eddie he would be able to quickly learn the business, Frank quit the plumbing trade, and he and his brother Eddie joined Jimmy in the auto body business.

As time went on, Frank became concerned about the amount of personal liability they all carried and suggested the three of them form a corporation for protection. As they were putting the organizational structure together, Jim suggested that his wife also be included as an officer of the corporation. This became a stumbling block for Frank.

Still not sold on the business idea and with a fifth child (Bobby) on the way in 1958, Frank made a decision to return to the plumbing trade.

Plumbing Reprise

This time Frank went to work as a superintendent or foreman for one of his dad's friends, a plumbing contractor named John Debelak. It was a good job for a good boss, but it wasn't long before Frank realized that even a foreman's paycheck wouldn't be enough to meet the needs of his growing family. Frank reached the conclusion that the only way he would ever be able to make the amount of money he needed to provide for his family in the way he wanted was to go into business for himself.

He gave John twelve months' notice and found him a replacement, Pat Higgins. John was supportive of Frank's decision, and the two men remained close friends.

CHAPTER 4

— ⚬ —

Blau Plumbing 1.0

WITH JUST $600 in working capital, Frank J. Blau Jr. opened Blau Plumbing Inc. in 1960, on the first day of February. It wasn't the best time to start a business. The country was headed into a recession that would persist well into 1961. Things were tough.

Luckily, Frank was, too. He converted his attached garage into an office and got to work.

In October 1960, a sixth child, John, was born.

Recalls Frank, "Not everyone thought I would make it. People said, 'You've gotta be kidding me, starting a business with six kids, in a recession? You're not going to be able to make it.' I told them, 'Don't be so sure. I'm gonna make it.'"

How could he be so sure? Frank says,

I said a good amount of prayers. I looked at my family and said, "I gotta make it." John Debelak, my previous employer who had become a friend, said, "You're gonna make it, but it will be tough."

There were moments of despair, times when the telephone didn't ring. But it was better than working for a paycheck. At first, I would get calls from customers at seven or eight o'clock at night, and I would take them. I'd work fourteen, fifteen, or sixteen hours a day. You do what you've got to do to survive.

Eventually, people started hearing about us. They heard that we'd go out on service calls at ten or eleven o'clock at night. Our best advertising came from people who experienced our service after they had called their regular plumber, who only wanted to provide service during normal hours. For us, normal hours were *all hours*. We were like doctors and nurses, taking care of people whenever they needed us.

CHAPTER 5

Searching for Knowledge

"ONE OF THE first things I did as a new business owner was to join the Milwaukee Plumbing Contractors Association (MPCA). I thought it would be a source of knowledge," recalls Frank.

Frank severed his individual union membership and joined as a contractor; he wanted to become a union employer.

"I went to their offices to introduce myself, and that caught them by surprise. They said most people didn't just show up," recalls Frank.

They—and ultimately the plumbing industry as a whole—would soon discover that Frank J. Blau Jr. was definitely not "most people." Frank soon discovered the association was more a social club than a source of education and information.

Over time Frank realized the various associations, including the national associations, were focused primarily on technical and political issues. In fact, when it came to making money in the plumbing business, no one knew anything. Frank still joined, but he now knew he would have to figure things out for himself.

Says Frank, "Just imagine a young, outspoken contractor, Frank Blau, approaching the executive director of the association he recently joined, telling him, 'We need a public relations committee because we are the only ones who realize we are professionals, and we need a business management committee so people had some place to go to learn how to run their business properly!'"

Frank recalls, "The career executive director of the MPCA at that time was a man named Ralph Weber. Ralph heard me out and then he said,

'Thanks for the idea. You can be the chairman of both of those committees.' I learned one thing that day, and that was when you ask an association director for something, you're going to be the chairman of it. If you open your mouth, you better accept it!"

Frank formed the business management committee, and they began offering seminars in markup. He also formed a public relations committee and catalyzed the development of a series of advertisements to change public opinion and position plumbing contractors as knowledgeable professionals.

They created a series of ads that ran in the *Milwaukee Journal* throughout the 1960s. One of them appears here.

In the meantime, Frank's dad, who had a few connections, introduced Frank Jr. to the super for the local telephone company. This led to his first big job, changing out washers in a series of commercial wall-hung toilets. To complete this job, Frank also had to hire his first union plumber.

The business continued to grow. Frank moved his office out of the kitchen and into a new three-car garage he'd built in his backyard.

CHAPTER 6

⸻ ❧ ⸻

Numbers Crunching

"THE FUNDAMENTALS OF Selling" was a ten-week course the PHCIB (Plumbing-Heating-Cooling Information Bureau) offered. Eager for any information he could use to build Blau Plumbing, Frank signed up for it.

Frank recalls, "The course was held at the Wisconsin Gas Company in downtown Milwaukee. Three hours per session, once a week for ten weeks. That is where I learned how to sell. Selling is a science, just like business. It is a mathematical science, numbers crunching."

As Frank learned about more about salesmanship, he realized it was going to be tough to sell from catalogs. He set a goal to create a

showroom, a place where customers could touch and feel the products. Frank still has the certificate.

In October 1961, Frank's seventh child, a daughter, Janet, was born.

It was an article on markup and margin that appeared in *Domestic Engineering* magazine in 1962, however, that changed everything for Frank. He recalls, "The markup and margin concept was so foreign to me at first that I read the article three times. But once I got it, I finally knew what I was doing when estimating my work."

Blau Plumbing was doing only new construction at the time. Frank's cost to do a simple house (time and materials) was $1,000, for which he charged $1,250. After crunching the numbers according to the formula in the article, Frank realized he really needed to charge $1,333.

Frank explains, "I was just as ignorant as everyone else. I'd been in business for about a year and a half at that point. The *Domestic Engineering* magazine article on margin and markup was the 'aha!' moment."

When Frank told his new construction builders he needed to raise his prices, he lost some of them over eighty-five dollars. Some builders derided him for even asking. "We'll replace you in a heartbeat," they jeered.

The issue of competitors who undercharged because they didn't understanding pricing, however, was only half of the equation. Frank knew the other half was that plumbing and the plumbing industry as a whole still had a serious public perception problem.

A few contractors stayed loyal to him; others hired estimators who found "slugs" (see below) to do the work.

For those who don't know, a slug is a type of snail. Snails are slow and primitive, so I used the term to describe people in our industry who fit that description. Most people regard snails/slugs as loathsome creatures—except for French chefs, who call them escargots and prepare them smothered in butter.

—Frank J. Blau Jr.

Understanding Markup — The Hypothetical Selling Price — a sample Frank Blau workshop exercise

If X Equals 100% of the Selling Price, calculate the Selling Price

Material &	15% Overhead
Labor Direct Cost	10% Net Profit

Materials & Labor Direct Cost	$1,000
Overhead Percentage	15%
Net Profit Desired	10%
Proper Selling Price = X =	$_____

Check Your Work:

Selling Price	$_____
Overhead Dollars	$_____
Net Profit Dollars	$_____
Total Overhead and Net Profit Dollars	$_____

Subtract overhead and net profit dollars from selling price. Correct answer should equal material and labor cost. $_____

Try it!

Hint: Think percentages, not numbers, and go to A1 Appendix for the answer.

CHAPTER 7

―――――∽――――――

Eddie

EDDIE, FRANK'S BROTHER, lived in Tampa, Florida, in 1963. Eddie already had a steam-cleaning business, but he had recently started a used-car business and had about twenty cars on his lot.

One night there was a deep freeze—in Florida. Half of the cars on the lot froze, and the engine blocks cracked. What a disaster. Back in Milwaukee, Frank was about to take on a partner—Pat Higgins—the man who had succeeded Frank as foreman at John Debelak's plumbing company. The papers were all drawn up, but then Frank heard about Eddie's problems, and he started thinking.

Recalls Frank, "At the time in Wisconsin, there was a lot of infrastructure building along the interstate, including large hotels. The plumbing for many of these buildings was being done by unlicensed contractors. To crack down on this, the state decided that for a limited time, anyone with a certain amount of experience could be grandfathered in as a licensed plumber, with no exam!"

Eddie was already a great mechanic. This was his chance. Frank called and asked him whether he wanted to join the business.

Says Frank, "I told him, 'Eddie, you'll have to trust me. You'll own fifty percent of the business. And you'll have a place to live, too.'"

Eddie packed up the family and was back in Milwaukee within three days. "It was perfect timing," recalls Frank. Thus began a business partnership that lasted thirty-three years.

Pat Higgins understood. He stayed with John Debelak for the rest of his career.

Frank and Eddie set about building the business. Frank emphasizes, "Without Eddie, Blau Plumbing wouldn't be nearly what it is today. He was a *supreme* marketer."

CHAPTER 8

❧

Showroom Time

IN THOSE EARLY days, Blau Plumbing primarily focused on new construction. As a subcontractor, the protocol is to mostly work through the general contractor, who then communicates with the people who own the house. Frank wanted an opportunity to work with those customers directly so he could sell them upgraded fixtures and make a bigger profit.

"Very early on, I realized that if I was going to be in business, I better have a showroom," Frank says.

In January 1963, Frank rented a twelve-hundred-square-foot store in town next to a barber shop and set up a modest showroom, achieving the goal he'd set at the end of 1961. Frank encouraged his builders to send their customers to the new facility—and they did.

"Mr. Blau has a beautiful showroom, and you'll have an opportunity to view the fixtures we will be installing," the builders said by way of introduction.

Once customers were in the showroom, Frank's objective was to upsell the fixtures. Instead of a round toilet, he showed them a nicer, more expensive elongated toilet and better-grade faucets.

The industry noticed. The following quotes are from a feature article published in the April 1, 1963, issue of *The Contractor* magazine.

Name brand merchandise is given prominence. Samples of top-quality name-brand bathroom fixtures are shown alongside lower-priced builders' numbers for direct comparisons. Both price ranges are always displayed in the same color, however.

"It is much easier to sell up customers when you let them compare both the better and lower-grade fixtures to the same color. It gives them a truer picture of the quality they can gain by spending a few more colors," said Blau.

To help particularly promising prospects visualize the end result, Frank hired a commercial artist to create a rendering of the finished remodeling project. The article says,

> Blau borrows a page from the books of builders and architects when he goes after a particularly promising prospect: he hires a commercial artist to draw a watercolor rendering of what the proposed bathroom installation will look like when completed.
>
> "Few people are able to visualize what a remodeled bathroom will look like when finished. It's difficult for many of us to picture how the colors will blend. That's where these watercolor renderings come in handy. They help prospects make up their minds about color combinations. And they also convince them that they are dealing with a competent contractor. The average customer will not question the quality of your bathroom fixtures. What they are seeking are qualified advice and decorating ideas. If you offer suggestions they instinctively feel are 'just right' for their bathroom installation, you've made a sale," said Blau.

Frank's goal with the showroom was also to position Blau Plumbing firmly in the minds of customers as a highly professional company. Again here's an excerpt from *The Contractor* article:

"'I try to give my customers the impression that they are dealing with a plumbing contractor who is also a businessman. This showroom and my office are selling tools,' said Blau."

In a 2010 article on Blau Plumbing's twenty-fifth anniversary, which appeared in *Plumbing & Mechanical* (*PM*) magazine, Frank's son Jim shared his recollection of one of the first plumbing trucks his father owned.

"'I remember cleaning the tools out of the old Suburban so we could put the seats back in the truck and go to church on Sunday,' Jim Blau says. The Milwaukee, Wis.-based company has come a long way since the days of being located next to John's Barber Shop where Jim, the current president of Blau Plumbing Inc., used to count inventory in the warehouse basement at night."

Lead Dog

During this time, Frank also developed and sold a few of his own properties. Says Frank,

> I made a deal with a builder friend, Bob DuCharm. I said, "You expedite the construction, and I'll pay you a percentage of my profit." He agreed.
>
> I purchased three lots in a nice location near a country club, and I put together a lovely custom house. Instead of traditional low-quality fixtures, the house included luxurious bathrooms, with high-grade toilets and even bidets. This way, I could break away from the pack and stand above the competition. When it was done, I put an ad in the paper.
>
> My builder friend went on vacation, and so that Sunday, I worked the open house. By four o'clock in the afternoon, I was getting ready to close it up, when a couple walked in the door.
>
> I gave them a tour of the house, and I could tell she wanted it. Bob and I had both agreed on a price for the home, but spontaneously I increased it by $30,000 and told him I wouldn't take a cent less. He said, "Where's the paperwork?"
>
> The problem was, I didn't have any.
>
> The man grabbed a yellow pad and wrote up an offer to purchase. I asked for $20,000 down, and he wrote me a check on the spot.
>
> When Bob got back from vacation, he was shocked to find out I'd sold the house for $30,000 more than the original asking price.
>
> I said to him, "See, I proved it to you. If you're not the lead dog in a pack of hounds, the scenery never changes."

I sold all three properties that way. I sat in the home and waited for the right buyers. I looked for people who had rings on their fingers and nicely heeled shoes.

Defending His Turf

Another area in which Frank excelled was in defending his position in the market. When specialty firms began to siphon off business Frank thought rightfully belonged with the plumbing contractor, he mounted a campaign that would position Blau Plumbing as the go-to contractor for ancillary upgrades, such as water softeners, garbage disposals, and water heaters.

Frank identified all potential sources of revenue and created strategies that enabled him to capture it all.

CHAPTER 9

Educating Everyone

HIS PRICES HAD to increase; that much Frank knew. But he competed against people whose prices were lower, and that fact made getting a job very difficult. "If I was going to make more money, I realized I would have to educate my competitors on what they need to be charging," says Frank.

Frank started teaching a business management course at the Milwaukee Plumbing-Heating Contractors Association (MPHCA). He also pushed the state contractors' association to work with the state to make business courses compulsory for the master plumber examination.

Here's an excerpt from the April 1, 1963, issue of *The Contractor*:

Frank introduced a resolution, unanimously approved, at the 1963 convention of the Wisconsin Association of Plumbing Contractors, which called for the association to work with state officials on setting up compulsory business courses for plumbing apprentices.

"Too many contractors fail as businessmen because of the inadequacy of their business training," says Blau.

"Our apprenticeship training is unrealistically lopsided in favor of technical instruction. Yet, we are all supposed to be able to develop into businessmen without being required to study the fundamental principles of successful contracting," says Blau.

In December 1963, Frank's eighth child, Mary, was born.

Postscript

As a result of that extensive feature in *The Contractor*, Frank received many inquiries. As always, he was very happy to share, in great detail, the design and structure of his programs, and he urged their adoption.

Frank's response to just one of those inquiries, in March 1964, appears below.

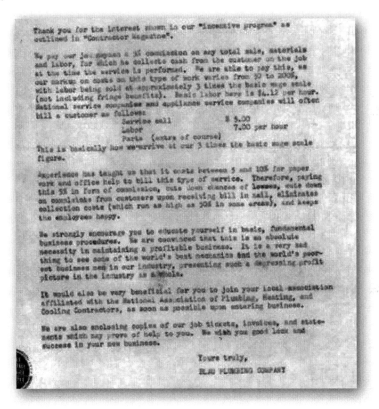

Public Image Maker

During this time, Frank also undertook many personal efforts to improve the public image of the plumbing industry. In one effort, Frank purchased two thousand booklets titled *The Story of Water Supply*, published by the American Water Works Association. He handed these out during presentations with the sisters to their eighth-grade science classes at the different Catholic grade schools in the area.

Image courtesy of http://www.mycomicshop.com.

"We received wonderful thank-you letters from parents for sending them, and we got a lot of mileage out of it as a PR effort," Frank recalls.

Home Show Home Run

In April 1964, Frank participated in the plans and execution of the plumbing center display for the MPCA Home Builder's Show, his first cooperative venture with the organization.

Frank received much positive feedback, including a merit award from the media. He also received a letter of appreciation from Don Wegner, then president of the MPCA.

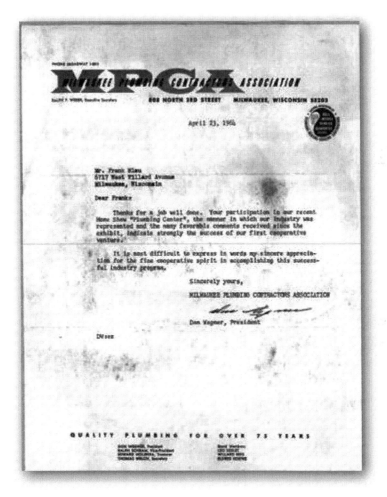

With Don Wegner, then president of the MPCA, and another contractor, Frank began presenting seminars on "The Business of Contracting" to elevate the knowledge of some of his fellow members.

Frank would ultimately be the president of the MPCA as well as the president of the Wisconsin Plumbing Contractors Association. He would be acknowledged as the contractor of the year for the state of Wisconsin.

CHAPTER 10

Schooling the Board

A FARMER NOMINATED Frank for president of the school board. The superintendent of schools called out, "Are there any other nominations?" There weren't. Frank was it.

This all started in 1964 when Frank and three other men campaigned for the ouster of four of the existing board members, whom they thought were out to lunch.

Recalls Frank, "At the time, Germantown wasn't even a K–12 district. There was no school board policy, nothing. People were encouraging me to run—we figured if all of us could get in, the others would lose, and we'd have a board of progressive thinkers. And we were elected."

The next step was to go over to the district offices and elect a school board president. The superintendent of schools explained that he'd ask three times for nominees. That's when a local farmer nominated Frank. The superintendent asked two more times. Frank was the only one nominated.

In one split second, Frank said to himself, "Frank, you asshole. You got yourself into this. Now step up!"

As he accepted the nomination, the superintendent slammed down the gavel and handed it to Frank, the new school board president. Frank's first act was to nominate the farmer for treasurer. Frank would serve as Germantown school board president for the next three years, overseeing a $10 million budget.

Pipe Scheme

Prior to being elected, Frank had had an agenda to expand the school system to better prepare students who were considering college. Frank and Irene made recommendations with the citizens committee and the Germantown school district, which included building a new high school. (Frank says he still has the plans.)

The assigned architectural firm solicited bids from plumbing contractors for the project. Frank knew the plumbing contractor who had won the bid and was seriously concerned, because his price was $150,000 less than the second bidder. He urged the board to hire an independent plumbing inspector to keep an eye on things.

The architectural firm suggested a particular service plumber. Frank objected vigorously. He knew the guy could barely read a blueprint. Unfortunately, the board didn't take his advice. They hired him anyway—to save money.

Frank realized he had no other choice but to monitor the project himself. He began stopping by the site every day after work. Since he had played a big part in specifying the plumbing, he knew what it should look like. For example, the plans called for oversized pipes to accommodate any future additions to the high school. The waste and vent pipes were to be "Byers pipe" with a one-hundred-year lifetime. Red spiral lines identified this pipe through all the length of the pipe.

One day as Frank walked around the site, he noticed the size of the drain lines. They didn't look right. He got in the ditch and measured. The pipe was two inches smaller than what was specified. Cheater!

Then, on one of the bathroom walls, Frank saw a vent pipe extending beyond the top of the bricks. He noticed the identifying red stripe on the pipe. But it just didn't look right. He became suspicious.

Frank went over to the pipe pile. As he dug through it, he discovered that inside the larger pipes were pipes that were two inches smaller in diameter. He also found a lot of galvanized pipe, instead of the longer-lasting Byers pipe, which had been specified.

He went back to the bathroom wall. Sure enough, the red stripe on the smaller pipe had been painted over with black paint. Frank thought, "We're getting a real screwing. That's one of the reasons the price was so low."

Frank took the school board to the job site and pointed out the discrepancies. A special school board meeting was called, with the public in attendance. Frank sat at the head of the table and wore sunglasses.

The contractor sent his son to represent him. Once confronted with the evidence, the contractor's son made excuses.

This response incensed Frank. He pounded his fist on the table, whipped off his glasses, and growled, "You're trying to bullshit everyone, but you can't bullshit me. You have been screwing us! And I have the evidence!"

The architect made the contractor tear out all the incorrect work, redo it at no cost to the city, and got the inspector fired, too. This was one of the reasons Frank decided to get involved in the school board and support Milwaukee education.

Discipline Dilemmas

As president of the school board, Frank often got calls from parents who complained about the lack of discipline in the schools. He advised them to follow the chain of command.

"'Talk to the teacher, the principal, and the superintendent. Then talk to me. If it's still an issue, I'll put you on the agenda.' But I'd also ask them, 'Are you sure you're not at fault? Have you taken the time? What are your habits? Most of the habits we practice are bad habits,'" recalls Frank. "Teaching kids to respect people and property starts with the parents. It starts with the third diaper change. That's mentoring."

Family Heartbreak

Steven Frances Blau was born in October 1966. He had a congenital heart condition.

"His little fingers were blue. His lips were blue," Frank says. "We knew something was wrong. He bravely endured two operations to correct the condition but still needed one more. Our doctor assured us that the procedure would go smoothly. After the surgery, Irene and I were spending the night at the hospital. At three in the morning, we were awakened by rushing feet and the realization that our child was in danger. Stevie died that night in May 1967."

William Steven Blau was born in 1970.

"Billy was the spitting image of Stevie," Frank says. "Irene and I compare baby pictures. They could have been twins. I give Irene so much credit for being an amazing mother and having endured so much heartbreak."

CHAPTER 11

Last Straw, Many Firsts

UPSTAIRS BEHIND THE altar, they were playing cards and drinking beer instead of working. That's how Frank found the job site foreman of the Mary Queen of Heaven Church rectory and school job during a routine visit. It was one of his biggest projects.

Frank remembers, "That was last straw. I closed the door and went to the car. Got Eddie on the CB radio and said, 'We are going full bore into service, and you are going to be our marketing guy.'"

It was 1971.

Advertising Pioneers

A plumbing service business would enable Frank and Eddie to deal directly with consumers, the ones spending the money. But first they needed to figure out how to get the phone to ring. They set out to do some advertising. He and Eddie came up with an ad.

"Our first ad was a spaceman with a rotor blade on his head sitting on a toilet. It was inspired by Kennedy's space program. We were very pleased with ourselves. Then the agency we contacted to place the ad told us no one would run an ad with a toilet. Toilets in advertising were verboten! We kept the Sudden Service line, but instead of a toilet, we put the guy in a bathtub. The rest is history," says Frank.

"Eddie is totally responsible for that one. Eddie also was the first guy to run a full-page ad in the Yellow Pages, when every other plumber merely added his company to the alphabetical list. He raised the bar on Yellow Pages advertising and a lot of service businesses, including a lot of our competitors, started to imitate what we were doing," recalls Frank.

Frank says Eddie had the ads all lined up, one after the other and well in advance of the due dates. Every year the competitors followed with the same ad, but Blau Plumbing owned the first position.

They pioneered the rolling billboard concept, now commonplace in the service industry. "We purchased large panel trucks for the mobile marketing effect they offered. Other contractors drove white trucks with no branding. We plastered our trucks with our logo, and bright red, white, and blue graphics and lettering," says Frank.

> Frank coined the unique selling proposition (USP) of "sudden service." He hired professionals to work on a logo and tested different logo concepts. To take advantage of the outer-space fever gripping the nation during the Kennedy administration, Frank and his brother settled on a spaceman in a bathtub with a helicopter rotor. Both the logo and the USP – have been imitated.
>
> —Matt Michel

More Firsts
Matt Michel, CEO of the Service Roundtable, is a Frank Blau devotee. He is quick to point out many other trails Frank J. Blau Jr. blazed.

> Frank was the first contractor to give his technicians handheld computers, which were loaded with the Blau price book. He also started the practice of valve tags. He developed a simple, efficient, and effective inventory control system. He created his own truck shelving system that maximizes inventory and simplifies inventory control.
>
> Maybe Frank's greatest innovation is also his simplest. He came to the revelation that plumbers, operating at the top of their

game, should be rewarded for their efforts. Not only should the owners be rewarded, Frank concluded, but also the plumbers and technicians who helped them earn their wealth.

Frank paid his people well, gave them and their families health insurance, and created profit sharing and fully funded retirement plans. If a plumber was to give Frank twenty to twenty-five years of service, Frank wanted him to be able to retire in comfort. His motives come from the heart. Frank chokes up when he talks about the wealth his employees managed to accumulate through his company.

Blau Plumbing continued to grow. By the end of 1973, the company head-quarters was located in a fourteen-thousand-square-foot facility with offices, a dispatch center, and a warehouse.

CHAPTER 12

~

Lived to Teach

FRANK ADMITS THAT his initial motivation to figure out how to be a successful businessman was based on selfish reasons. "Initially, the reason I wanted to educate competition was so I could have it little easier," Frank recalls. But the last of three close calls with death in 1974 shifted his point of view forever.

"After the third time I cheated death, I realized there was a reason I was still here," recalls Frank. "There was no one like me. I learned all this the wrong way. I saw the ignorance all around me. I knew business was a mathematical science—regardless of the industry. Something had to be done, and done by me."

Given the gravity of these events, stepping aside and letting Frank tell you these stories himself seems appropriate.

Cheating Death at Washington Island—1946

The first time, my dad and a friend of mine, Zeke, were up at Washington Island, which is about seven miles off the tip of the Door Peninsula. You could catch big fish there, big northern pike. We were staying at the Idables, a lodge near the water. It was late in the afternoon, Memorial Day weekend, and still cold out.

My dad, Zeke, and I rented a rowboat with a motor at Detroit Harbor and went out fishing. At the time, I was seventeen years old, a year from graduating from high school.

All of a sudden, the water got rough. Pa said, "Time to go back into shore." Except that was where the waves were coming from.

Water starting coming over the bow, and we did sink.

My friend Zeke didn't know how to swim a stroke, but I did. I was trying to keep both Zeke and me afloat, but he was panic stricken and started to fight. I said, "Let go! We're both going to drown!" He couldn't, so I popped him one. I was an athlete in good shape, so I was able to control him.

We were able to turn over the boat so there was an air pocket underneath. We started to yell, "One, two, three—help!" But we quickly realized it wasn't going to do any good.

Our voices kept getting carried away from shore, which was a mile away at this point.

I said, "Pa, I'm going to have to make shore if there is any chance." I took off my heavy corduroy pants and started swimming.

My target was a house with a bright light, dead reckoning. When I started out, it was light, and so I continued on swimming toward that light. Every time I was about ready to go under, I thought, I'm too young to die!

Finally, I felt earth under me. I stumbled back to Idables. I came through the door and got right up to their big cast-iron cooking stove and burned myself.

The owners, Mr. and Mrs. Einerson, were having dinner and celebrating their anniversary, with nice champagne.

They poured some of the champagne down my throat and called the doctor who lived on the island, who rushed over to see me.

I was in shock but with it enough to tell them there were two more out there. The Einersons called the coast guard, who went out and rescued my father and my friend.

Cheating Death by Train—1959

The second time I cheated death, I was about thirty years old. I was on my way to attend a sales course at Plumbing Heating-Cooling

Information Bureau in downtown Milwaukee and was engrossed in thinking about that.

And I drove my '54 Buick right into the engine of a Schlitz beer train—eighty cars full of beer out of Milwaukee. I hadn't seen any blinking lights at the crossing.

As the train dragged my car down the track, the driver door popped open, and I popped out, physically unharmed, even though I had almost killed myself.

It took the engineer one hundred yards or longer to stop the train. He was pissed. He said, "This was my last run, and I'm retired, you SOB!"

Pretty soon a motorcycle cop drove up. I had to think fast. I told him, "The signals didn't come on in time!"

The cop said, "I'm going to cite you for failure to yield the right of way. Be at the DA's office in Milwaukee on this date."

Not sure what to expect, I got a neck brace and went to court. The engineer and another guy, an attorney, were there dressed in suits. I said, "I was on my way to downtown Milwaukee and never saw any signals. I'm lucky to be alive!"

The railroad attorney had a briefcase that contained a type-writer. He wanted me to sign a release that I wasn't hurt.

I said, "I didn't feel hurt, and I would be happy to sign a release, if it would take effect after ninety days." Then I said, "One other thing: my car is totaled, so I don't have a car."

They brought the papers.

Cheating Death in the Gulf—1974

The last time I outran the grim reaper was on a boat in the Gulf of Mexico, deep-sea fishing for grouper and red snapper with my brother Eddie and my son Tommy on Eddie's boat, a thirty-eight-footer named the *Pipe Dream*.

We were about fifty miles from shore and catching lots of fish, when suddenly sharks appeared. Our rods went limp, and all that was left of the grouper we'd hooked was the head. We already had about nine hundred pounds on board at that point, and so we decided to go in. We headed east, with Eddie piloting the boat.

I was sitting in the back of the boat, my feet up on the transom, watching this big, beautiful sunset. Then I thought, Something is wrong. The sun is getting higher instead of going down. We are sinking!

We opened up the bilge, and there was water in the boat. The batteries were also underwater.

Was the radio still working? Yes!

I got out a Mayday. The St. Petersburg Coast Guard responded, and I gave them a good fix as to where we were.

We started throwing fish overboard, and the sharks were right there. It was a feeding frenzy. I was sure that was it. I started saying the act of contrition.

In the meantime, Eddie felt around underwater in the bilge and found that a pipe had let loose. We had extra parts on board, so as we threw fish overboard, Eddie fixed the pipe and got the bilge pumped out.

I spotted the helicopter and tried to fire the flare. I hollered at my brother, "Eddie, it doesn't work!"

He said, "Gimme the goddamn gun!" He looked at it and said, "Frank, you #$%^$%! You got the shell in backward!"

In the end, we saved ourselves and the boat, too.

Why have I escaped death? It is so the next generation is better and smarter. Mom said, "Share what you've learned with your fellow man." There's a reason I'm still here. The good Lord planned it this way. I could have been gone a long time ago.

CHAPTER 13

꠷

Of Seminars and Slugs

"The Business of Contracting" seminars continued to grow in popularity, and by the mid-1970s, in addition to leading Blau Plumbing, Frank traveled the country, teaching, mentoring, and impelling contractors to "take the medicine" and join him in raising their ability to make a successful living.

Frank also continued efforts to raise public awareness of the vital importance of the home services industry in protecting the health, safety, and welfare of our nation. For some contractors, however, "the medicine" was a pill too bitter for them to swallow, and Frank wasn't known for candy coating. Then, as now, he calls things as he sees them.

The Real Deal

Frank never expected anyone to take what he said at face value, especially when it was something that was so challenging to every aspect of the way he or she did business. To prove to people they could trust what he said, Frank showed his W-2s and balance sheets at the beginning of class.

Frank says, "I asked myself, 'What am I going to do, when speaking to people for first time, to prove I'm not blowing smoke out my you-know-what?' I figured I would show my W-2s to prove I was not a BSer, so people would listen to me. I'd say, 'Here's the proof, and you can do it too.'"

Many people objected to Frank's advice, and his approach made others feel downright threatened. They went to great lengths to protest against Frank's message.

A Slug by Any Other Name
Frank recalls,

One time a fellow who used to work for Blau Plumbing in Milwaukee turned up at a seminar I was giving in Montreal. This guy had always been offended by my use of the word *slug*.

In the middle of the morning session, the fellow suddenly stood up and came toward me. Once he was in front of me, he ripped his dress shirt open. On his undershirt was a big slug in a red circle with a slash through it—a no-slug sign!

Then he started yelling at me. At first, we all thought it was a joke, but then we realized he was serious. His classmates got protective and tackled him. Security took him away, and they had security at my class in the afternoon.

I'd tried everything to educate him, but this fellow still thought my methods for making a good living meant ripping people off. It's about more than the money. Emotions run high.

Every Living Creature Contributes
Says Frank,

Every living creature makes a contribution. We are food for others at the very least. What about your contribution? How about compared to McDonalds? Sure, they fill us full of cholesterol, but they also provide lots of jobs and teach good work habits. Compared to attorneys? Compared to most plumbing-heating-cooling (PHC) contractors? Think about it—as PHC contractors, *we protect the public health.*

Understand that everything that lives on this earth makes a contribution. Compare all these contributions to what it is we really do.

CHAPTER 14

Leading Change

THE RECESSION HIT, and by 1983, a lot of plumbers were out of work. Most contractors had started their businesses before building supplies were so readily available to consumers; now anyone could buy supplies from Home Depot, Lowe's, and Menards. To save money, many people were opting to do work themselves rather than hiring someone else to do it.

Rather than fight the DIY trend, Blau Plumbing embraced it. "Blau Plumbing: Showing, Selling, Excelling," an article Carole Pomerantz wrote for the April 1985 issue of *Plumbing & Mechanical* magazine, describes this in detail.

> The eighteen-hundred-square-foot repair parts center located in the lower level of the company's new forty-five-hundred-square-foot showroom [is] an area that is devoted to the do-it-yourselfer. Not only does it feature parts and hardware; it also has a video-tape library on how to install product.
>
> "First of all," [Frank] says, "we're moving product. Second, we can give the customer expert advice. We also tell the customer that if he or she can't complete the job, he or she knows Blau Plumbing will back him or her up." In over 75 percent of the cases, Blau maintains, "They can't complete the job and have to call us anyway!"

This all-in innovative approach was consistent with Frank's approach to everything undertaken and his reputation as someone who covers every base and attends to every detail.

Another area in which Frank managed change was in the company. Early on, he began grooming three of his sons to take over the business. In 1995, Frank handed off managerial duties to his sons at Blau Plumbing, becoming chairman of the company's board. His official retirement was in 2000.

Most people, freed from day-to-day responsibilities of their businesses, would go fishing. But Frank wasn't "most people." Instead he redoubled his efforts to educate anyone in the industry who would listen on the business of contracting.

CHAPTER 15

Blue-Collar Philosopher

FRANK BECAME A columnist for *Plumbing & Mechanical* magazine in 1985. Over the years Frank and its editorial director, Jim, formed a close relationship, which continues to this day. Jim recalls,

> I was introduced to Frank in the mideighties by the original publisher of *PM* magazine, Jerry Tucker. He had seen and met Frank at a kitchen and bath convention, and thought he'd make a good addition.
>
> Although Frank's focus was on number crunching, his influence went beyond that. He was a blue-collar philosopher, someone who not only knew numbers and had a mission but who also was a class warrior in the best sense of the word.
>
> Frank would always say that there was no reason why blue-collar people, plumbers, HVAC contractors, people who provide the joys of modern civilization, shouldn't enjoy a good life, like those who wore a shirt and tie. And he hammered home that message continuously.
>
> Every column had the same underlying messaging, which was, "Stand up for yourself; you deserve to make more money. Don't let people look down on you."
>
> We started with a cover story on his company, a feature article on successful plumbing contractors, and out of that a regular column arose.

In 1989, Frank wrote the column "How Much Should a Contractor Charge?" which was a turning point for many contractors.

Over the course of sixteen years, Frank wrote two columns, Business Tips and The Business of Contracting, which were dedicated to educating, inspiring, and providing hope and a way to a better life for thousands of fellow contractors.

Frank's farewell column appeared in *PM* magazine on February 1, 2003. You can read all Frank's *PM* columns and more in the book *The Business of Contracting*, available at ShuBee.com. Here's the link: http://www.shubee.com/frank-blau-in-business-of-contracting-in-workbook.html.

For the thousands of contractors whose lives Frank's work had already changed, it was truly the end of an era. What they didn't know was that the best was yet to come.

CHAPTER 16

Expert Witness

AN ATTORNEY WAS looking for an expert witness for his client, a plumbing and mechanical contractor whose partner was suing him. He called Frank.

"He said his client had been reading my columns in *Plumbing & Mechanical* magazine and thought I might be able to help them out," recalls Frank.

An attorney explained the situation to Frank. The contractor, Andy (not his real name), was part owner of a large mechanical company in Racine, Wisconsin. The company had recently opened another office in Phoenix, where there was a lot of new construction going on, especially commercial.

Andy had moved to Phoenix to work on the business, and his partner was supposed to come and help out, except that he didn't. His excuse was that he was having marital problems.

In the meantime, the Phoenix office took off. To keep up with everything, Andy worked day and night, doing everything from estimating to creating plans to hiring superintendents. On top of that, he worked for peanuts.

So one day, Andy decided to cut himself a paycheck for a salary commensurate to what he should have received, which was in the low six figures. He took it as compensation and paid taxes on it.

However, when his partner back in Wisconsin saw how much the paycheck was, he didn't see it as commensurate; he saw it as embezzlement and filed suit under the RICOH Act.

Andy hired an attorney, who asked whether he knew anyone who could be an expert witness. Andy said, "There's a guy that writes for *PM* magazine. He might be your guy." And the attorney called Frank.

Frank heard the attorney out and said, "Let me get back to you." Frank's first call was to *his* attorney, Dick Pitzner, who also was a CPA. Frank said to him, "You think I can do it?"

Dick said, "Frank, you would make a great expert witness. I am going to give you some advice. Tell him you are going to charge ten thousand dollars up front. Tell them you want to meet in Milwaukee. You don't want to fly to Phoenix; you want them to come here."

Frank did this and included expenses, too. A check was arranged. Both firms agreed to meet in the boardroom of the Ramada Inn in Milwaukee, and they secured two adjoining rooms for lawyer/client conferences.

On the day of the meeting, Frank, the contractor, and his two attorneys were face-to-face with four high-powered Milwaukee attorneys wearing expensive shoes and custom-made suits.

Frank, who was in a sport coat and tie, was sandwiched between the Phoenix attorneys and their client. The four opposing attorneys immediately started trying to discredit Frank. "What makes you an expert witness?" said one of them. They were testing him.

Frank explained that he was an educator and a successful Milwaukee businessman. He then took four packets of stapled worksheets out of his portfolio and passed them out to the attorneys.

"Let me give you an example," said Frank, who then led the men through the hypothetical selling price exercise and invited them to try it for themselves. All four came up with the same answer—$1,250.

"Gentlemen, you all came up with the most popular *incorrect* answer," said Frank, who then proceeded to give them a mini-seminar.

As soon as Frank had finished, the lead attorney for the Phoenix contractor kicked Frank in the shin and said, "I'd like to caucus."

Once they were in the other room, he said, "Frank, you SOB. You just got 'em! You trapped them!" The opposing attorneys had tried to discredit Frank, and Frank had turned the tables on them.

Having established his credibility, Frank's offered his expert opinion, which was that if that fellow was wearing all the hats—estimator, foreman, and manager—he was entitled to all the salaries. If he'd had to pay someone a full salary for each position, the expense would actually have cost more than what he had drawn.

Frank suggested that the contractor admit some fault, take a bit of a hit, and put the thing to bed. The suit ended up being settled for a fraction of the initial figure. The whole matter was over in less than two hours.

CHAPTER 17

―❦―

Food within Reach

"PROCESSIONARY CATERPILLARS" IS what Frank calls contractors who insist on continuing to charge what everyone else is charging, even though they are starving as a result of that behavior.

> Processionary caterpillars get their name from their behavior. In the center of the flowerpot: food. Yet they follow each other around and around the edge of the pot. After ten days, they all die with food within reach.

> —Frank J. Blau Jr.

The flowerpot reference is to an 1896 experiment by French naturalist Jean-Henri Fabre.

The processionary caterpillar Frank refers to is the pine processionary caterpillar, a voracious insect found in the warmer regions of Southern Europe, the Near East, and North Africa.

In his experiment, Fabre took a large flowerpot and placed a number of caterpillars in single file around the circumference of the pot's rim. Each caterpillar's head touched the caterpillar in front of it (this is how they know to follow).

Fabre then placed the caterpillars' favorite food in the middle of the pot. Each caterpillar followed the one ahead without thinking. Round and round the edge of the flower pot they went for seven days; then one after the other they dropped dead from exhaustion and starvation, even though there was plenty of food just six inches away.

Interestingly, in addition to their long head-to-tail processions, described in the experiment above, these caterpillars are covered with articulating hairs that can sting and cause great discomfort to anyone who tries to mess around with them. Good thing Frank has thick skin.

CHAPTER 18

———— ✂ ————

Scratch Golfer

FRANK'S LIFETIME LOW golf score is 66 achieved on the par-71 course at North Hills Country Club in Menomonee Falls, Wisconsin, north of Milwaukee. To shoot five under par in golf is pretty remarkable in and of itself, but considering that Frank had never picked up a golf club until he was thirty-three years old, the score borders on phenomenal.

Frank's prowess at golf was remarkable and even phenomenal, but to those who knew him, it was hardly surprising. Also, at a time when golf club membership was considered a luxury outside the reach of trades-people, Frank maintained his membership for forty-eight years.

Like everything Frank decided to undertake, he drove tirelessly toward mastery. And not only did golf reignite his competitive drive to win; Frank quickly discovered that he still hated to lose.

For Frank and his good friend John Debelak, golf provided a way to get away from business for a day and talk about things. At Frank's suggestion they borrowed a set of clubs and headed to the local public golf course. It wasn't long before Frank and John blocked out the day and played seven to eight hours of golf.

Both men took lessons and learned about the game—not only the mechanics but also the mental components. Wanting to be able to play the better courses, Frank and John joined a country club but not the same one.

John joined Tuckaway Country Club, located in Franklin, south of Milwaukee; and Frank went north to Menomonee Falls and joined North Hills Country Club. The two of them then exchanged courtesies.

Golfing in Scotland

Members of Contractors 2000, now Nexstar, soon learned Frank was an avid golfer, and Nexstar member Kevin Shaw approached membership with a plan to send Frank and a few family members to Scotland, the birthplace of golf.

They flew out of the Minneapolis airport, and Dave Volgelesang, longtime Nexstar member and friend, was there to meet them and give everyone a proper send-off. Recalls Frank, "It was time to get on the plane when Dave handed me an envelope and instructed me not to open it until we were up in the air."

All were eager to find out what the envelope contained, so once they were airborne, Frank opened it. Inside was a letter and $500 in cash. Nice!

Says Frank, "I read that letter and started to cry. Dave had expressed his appreciation for me and all I had done to help him change his life. He was a shy fellow and not one to share his feelings, which made the letter even sweeter. Then my son-in-law read it, and he started to sob. He passed it onto my son Billy, who read it and sobbed, too. Then came Johnny, another son. People were starting to wonder what was going on up in first class. The flight attendant came over to see what the trouble was. We handed her the letter to read, and she started sobbing, too!"

The Blau party flew into Amsterdam (Frank: "You know that city where they sell sex on the street?"), then progressed on to Scotland.

Recalls Frank, "We had one hell of a time. We played St. Andrews and at least seven courses total in a week-and-a-half period. It was an experience of a lifetime, and I owe it all to the generous Nexstar membership. They didn't have to do it."

Students Are Where You Find Them

During one golf game in Scotland, Frank talked to his caddie and found out he was a mason, a bricklayer. Frank asked him, "How come you're not brick laying instead of caddying?" After golf, they went for libations, and as they relaxed, Frank talked to the caddie and laid the hypothetical selling price job on him. Of course, the caddie failed the test.

When Frank got back to the States and to his office, he sent the caddie/mason *The Business of Contracting* set on video. In gratitude, the caddie/mason sent Frank a nice Scottish wool tie.

Coincidentally, another gentleman he was caddying for owned a construction company in the United States that was building a hospital, and that guy hired him as a superintendent mason. Frank's former caddie works and lives in the United States now. He told Frank he owes his success as a mason and manager to his intervention.

For Frank this was just another day in the life of a man whose mission is to share what he's learned with his fellow man so every generation must have it better than the previous generation.

CHAPTER 19

Defending Flat Rate

ASSISTANT EXECUTIVE DIRECTOR of the Minnesota Plumbing-Heating-Cooling Contractors Association (MPHCCA), Jack Tester, had heard about Frank J. Blau Jr., and in 1990 he brought Frank to teach "The Business of Contracting" seminar to his members. The seminars were a big hit with the contractors, and many MPHCCA members immediately adopted Frank's flat rate business model.

This aggravated some competitors who were still charging based on time and materials. And in their excitement, the newly converted may have initially come across as a little arrogant. Once they'd "taken the medicine," as Frank called it, the contractors couldn't understand why others wouldn't follow their lead. To them it just made sense.

The Time &Material (T&M) folks, who either didn't understand or agree with the rationale of the new business model, thought the "flat raters" were just out to screw the customer and other contractors, though nothing could have been further from the truth. Enough people complained, however, that eventually Hubert Humphrey Jr., then Minnesota attorney general, got wind of it.

Jack Tester had since left the PHCC but was notified that the attorney general had launched an inquiry. Jack immediately called Frank to warn him that he would likely be getting a call. Frank immediately called his attorney, Dick Pitzner, who told him, "Frank, if you get a call from him, tell him you won't speak with him unless I'm on the phone with you. You can handle anything, Frank!"

Frank did get the call and arranged a date and time for a three-way phone conference: Frank and Dick together on one line in Frank's office and Hubert Humphrey Jr. on the other. Frank said, "Your Honor, I'll tell you what I do. I try to create a proper intelligent selling price to benefit the state. I don't tell people what to charge. Would you like an example, like my students?"

Why, yes, he would, said the attorney general, so Frank walked him through the hypothetical selling-price exercise. At the end, Frank said, "Your Honor, you came up with the most popular incorrect selling price, which is one thousand two hundred fifty dollars."

"Well, if that is not the selling price, then what should it be?" asked Humphrey. Frank then explained how to get the correct answer.

"Not knowing how to set a correct selling price is why, out of one hundred businesses that start on the same day, you're lucky to have five make it to the five-year mark, Your Honor," counseled Frank.

The attorney general said he understood, and after a few follow-up calls, the matter was dropped.

The experience left an impression on Frank, however. His intent was to help contractors change for the better, but due to ignorance or envy, the old guard still attacked the new model, and its sole aim was to enable contractors, who were great mechanics, to obtain the knowledge needed to operate a sustainable and profitable contracting business. Explains Frank,

> What happens is that a kid learns a trade, and he finds an employer. He's young and single with no responsibilities. He starts at a certain rate. Then he gets married. He's still making the same money, but he and his wife get by.
>
> Then the kids start coming. The expenses increase, so the guy goes to his boss and asks for a raise. He says, "Boss, when you hired me, what I was earning at the time was perfect. Now I have a lot of financial responsibilities, and I need to make more money."
>
> The problem is, the slug he's working for may be the best mechanic, but he's also the worst businessman. So the boss says, "Sorry, kid, things are tough. We can't give you a raise." The guy

still needs a raise, so he goes and gets a job with someone else. He soon finds out there *is* no better place to work and earn more money, because *everyone is the same*!

To increase his income, he has no other choice but to go into business. But the problem there is that he doesn't know anything either, so it's another generation of starving plumbers.

On the other side, the boss is his own worst enemy, because he's just forced his employee to quit and start his own business, creating even more competition. We have met the enemy, and he is us.

There was still much work to be done.

[When] Frank put on one of his seminars, he would show people how much money he made last year—a six-figure salary, money that no one in that room was coming close to making.

He overheard one contractor say, "Ain't a plumber in the world worth $100K a year," and that statement is emblematic of the mentality Frank has battled over the years. He has always known the real problem is that contractors don't believe they deserve anything.

Frank's W-2 was proof that it could be done, and he had done it, that he was the real deal. It was the only reason he could think of that they should listen to him.

Go into any big market these days, call on plumbing contractors, and all are doing flat rating. It's really becoming the standard.

—Jim Olsztynski
Former publisher, *Plumbing & Mechanical* magazine

CHAPTER 20

———— ✺ ————

Blau and Brazil

THE BUSINESS OF Contracting and Business Tips, two regular columns Frank had been writing for *Plumbing & Mechanical* magazine since 1987, caught the attention of a man on the West Coast named George Brazil. George Brazil was a fellow contractor who was doing something in California that was similar to what Frank was doing in Milwaukee. The auto industry, the General Motors Mr. Goodwrench program, had also inspired his approach.

The Mr. Goodwrench program required each dealer's service department to adhere to a strict set of service delivery standards—high levels of factory training, keeping parts on hand, service department amenities—and flat rate pricing.

George contacted Frank and invited him to do seminars out West. While Frank was a relentlessly practical innovator focused on making money today, George's ideas were more bleeding edge and harder to monetize. Both men were forces of nature. Together, they were a force to be reckoned with.

Frank and George were also 100 percent aligned in their belief in elevating the image and performance of the mechanical contracting profession and shared a deep conviction that *this must happen*. This common goal would serve as the foundation for an enduring and very dear friendship.

NAPHCC No Go

Looking for more national reach, Frank, George, and another contractor, Mike Diamond, wanted to offer the seminar through the National

Association of Plumbing-Heating-Cooling Contractors (NAPHCC) but couldn't get traction. Similar to its regional chapters, the national association at that time was primarily a social organization, so meeting the needs and desires of the members who needed education about how to run their businesses wasn't a priority for them either.

In an attempt to address this oversight, George and Frank went to the NAPHCC and formed a committee to study the needs of the members. A few months later, they presented their findings to the NAPHCC board of directors and proposed an idea they called "The Traveling College of Knowledge."

Despite the new evidence that their members wanted and needed business training, the board wasn't interested. Frank was livid. "Not interested? Then I'm going to run for office," he decided.

He traveled around the country on his own dime, expressing his platform at state conventions and giving interviews to the press. Frank says, "I had supporters around the country. My dear friend George Brazil said, 'I'll support the living daylights out of you and pray that you lose.' He said, 'Frank, those guys will drive you crazy, and you'll never get to implement your programs. You'll be wasting time in meetings and getting nothing done.'"

After spending months on the road and $25,000 of his own money campaigning, Frank lost at the convention in New York. He recalls, "That got me pissed. I decided that if there was no way to make progress within the national organization, we would have to form one of our own."

CHAPTER 21

───── ✣ ─────

Contractors 2000 to Nexstar

CONVINCING GEORGE BRAZIL to start a new organization took time, but Frank finally sold him on the idea, and the two began envisioning an entity that would compete with the NAPHCC.

Recalls Frank, "George suggested that we test-market it in San Diego County because that's where a lot of products were test-marketed by manufacturers. I said, 'That's bullshit. We're going to test-market it all over the United States. We'll make it available to everyone with the simple message: "Join with us and learn how to make money." We know if we use that tagline, that'll get them. Our organization will take off like a rocket, thrive, and last from now until eternity. We will teach contractors how to make money.'"

To prove the concept of a traveling college of business knowledge, Frank invited a few contractors to stay a few days after a seminar he was doing in Clark, New Jersey, in June 1992. New Jersey contractor Dan Weltman was intrigued and decided to stay and explore Frank's ideas about starting a new organization, as did several other contractors who came to the seminar.

Frank had brought in a facilitator, and the group talked and talked. At the end of three days, there were lots of ideas, but nothing much had been finalized. Frank was afraid they would lose it all. Frank says, "I told everyone, 'Take out your calendars. We'll meet again in August at Blau Plumbing in Milwaukee, and bring your checkbooks.'" To fund the organization, each member would be asked to ante up.

One thing that *had* been decided in New Jersey was the name: Contractors 2000. (Fun fact: Richard Trethewey of *This Old House* also attended and came up with the name. He said it sounded progressive.)

When the group reconvened in Wisconsin, it was a matter of putting together the pieces and electing a president, chairman, and board of directors. Recalls Frank, "Everyone wanted me to become president, but I didn't want that. I wanted to be able to sit back and observe with my mouth shut, except when I thought it needed to be open."

The good news was that the original founders were full of passion and energy for the mission, but it took some time and effort to get everyone heading in the same direction.

A Fifty-Fifty Chance

Not everyone was convinced that the new organization would fly. Even Jim Olsztynski, then publisher of *Plumbing & Mechanical* magazine and someone who knew Frank well, thought it had only a fifty-fifty chance of succeeding.

In fact, Jim says he vividly remembers that first meeting, held in an upstairs training/conference room at Blau Plumbing in Wisconsin, with about twenty contractors present.

> After that meeting was over, I told Frank, "This is never going to fly!" It was disorganized, a cacophony of different ideas, with one person loudly objecting to everything. Total chaos. Three hours later, I walked away from the meeting, thinking it was a complete waste of time.
>
> But Frank called a subsequent meeting, which I didn't attend, and apparently he got organized and got commitments, and he and George Brazil took charge. Frank and George had such strong personalities; they at least stayed focused on the mission, and those not on board with it eventually drifted away. So began the organization that became Contractors 2000 and now is Nexstar.
>
> Out of this chaos, however, came a new order and an effective organization. And among its alumni are some of the most successful plumbing and HVAC contractors in the country.

Jim also points out how the changes in the industry increased Frank's sense of urgency when it came to spreading the concept of flat rate pricing.

Jim says, "Most plumbing contractors were charging twenty to forty dollars per hour, which didn't even cover overhead, and so a lot of them were jacking up prices on the materials, but that was getting harder to do with the advent of DIY stores, such as Home Depot."

Flat rate pricing enabled contractors to charge what they needed to charge to professionalize the service. From a customer standpoint, everyone wanted to know how much a service was going to cost before he or she said yes, so in that way, quoting a flat rate price removed his or her anxiety.

Although flat rate pricing was already being used in the automotive industry, others in the industry accused both Frank and George, being pioneers, of being "rip-off artists."

Both fought against the industry's hangdog mentality and most contractors' beliefs that they were undeserving of making money. Frank's message was "Take pride in what you do. You deserve to make a decent living, to be able to pay for your kid's college and retire, just like the white-collar worker does."

In November 1992, Frank Blau, George Brazil, and that group of pioneering contractors formed Contractors 2000, a member-owned organization dedicated to the education of the residential home service industry.

Someone had to teach folks how to make money and market their goods and services, and the mission of Contractors 2000 was to do just that.

Ass, Grass, and Lawn Mower

Frank's intent from the get-go was for Contractors 2000 to be self-sufficient, with his role being one of guide and adviser; he didn't want to be the group's president, so he had to select one.

Many widely expected that one of the founding members would be named, but Frank, unafraid of pissing people off to get to the right decision, changed his mind at the last minute and selected Jack Tester, former assistant executive director of the Minnesota PHCC, as the organization's first president instead.

After this announcement, Frank wasted no time in making his expectations clear.

> Frank leaned into me and said, "If you make a mistake, your ass is grass, and I'm the lawn mower." He was determined that Contractors 2000 be successful. That was real clear to me.
>
> —Jack Tester

By the end of 1998, Contractors 2000 was a growing member-owned organization that was well staffed with a strong working board and over 250 members.

> I gave Frank my check for four thousand dollars to join Contractors 2000. When I got the check back in my bank statement, it had tear stains on it—mine! It was a leap of faith.
>
> —Ellen Rohr

Jack Tester left the organization in 1998 to pursue another opportunity and passed the mantle of president to its next leader. After a couple of missteps, the organization floundered for leadership until the board of directors tapped Greg Niemi.

Greg led Contractors 2000 to overcome its growing pains and evolve into a thriving business networking organization that delivers comprehensive business training, proven business systems, and dedicated business coaching to independent home service plumbing, heating, air-conditioning, and electrical professionals.

This organization has been known since 2004 as the Nexstar Network.

Frank, you are a national treasure. You've got the fight of a badger, the tenacity of a snapping turtle, and the heart of a lion. And yes, you are one of my true, honest-to-goodness heroes.

—Denny Smith, president
Paul E. Smith Co. Inc.

CHAPTER 22

— ❧ —

The Next Generation

IN MANY WAYS 2004 was a watershed year. Contractors 2000 become known as the Nexstar Network, and Frank transferred ownership of Blau Plumbing Inc. to his sons Jim and Bobby, a huge achievement. However, the completion of this long-term goal meant that while Blau Plumbing would continue to be a member of Nexstar, Frank, one of its most revered founders, would not.

In May 2005, to recognize Frank's contribution, Nexstar's board passed a resolution, making him a lifetime member. Greg Niemi, then president and COO of Nexstar, said, "Although we won't be collecting dues from Frank anymore, we will look forward to collecting many more ideas, stories, and testimonials from him."

(achrnews.com/articles/96610-blau-honored-with-lifetime-membership-in nextar)

The Nexstar Legacy Foundation

In November 2005, Nexstar Legacy Foundation's newly elected board of trustees designated Frank Blau Jr. as honorary chairperson of the Nexstar Legacy Foundation. He was also awarded a lifetime membership to that organization.

The mission of the Nexstar Legacy Foundation, which a group of Nexstar members endowed, is to provide a channel for people in the home services industry to give back to their community.

As of October 2014, the Nexstar Legacy Foundation has given over $250,000 in scholarships to students. It also offers many programs specifically for our veterans, helping them find meaningful, lucrative careers in the trades (in other words, plumbing, heating, cooling, and electrical industries).

The Nexstar Network and the Legacy Foundation share what they have learned from Frank with their fellow men and women, thereby extending Frank's commitment to ensuring that the next generation must have it better than the last.

Completing the Circle

Jack Tester returned to Nexstar in 2006, initially as an independent business coach. He says he always knew he'd be coming back someday. "It really did feel like coming home," says Jack. In November 2011, Jack Tester became the organization's current president.

> What Frank started in 1992, an organization focused solely on helping members grow profitably still resonates today, with over five hundred contractors enjoying the benefits of Nexstar.
>
> —Jack Tester
> President, Nexstar Network

With the future of his family and his legacy secure, Frank turned his attention to his Whitetail Ranch.

CHAPTER 23

Whitetail Ranch

FRANK ASSEMBLED 135 acres of prime woodland in Black River Falls, Wisconsin, to create Whitetail Ranch in the early 2000s. On this property, Frank built a hunting cabin and established a premier white-tailed deer reserve and hunting facility.

On a typical weekend, Frank's boys and "grand boys" head up to the ranch on Friday, arriving in the early afternoon. Frank makes chili for dinner, and there is beer, wine, whiskey, and rum. Everyone hits the sack early so he can get up at four thirty in the morning to go hunting.

Frank recalls, "As a young man, I loved to fish and hunt. Now, I have the time and resources to develop this property and introduce my family to the joys of outdoor life and proper wildlife management."

Deer Biologist and Fanatical Farmer

As a result, Frank is now a student of deer hunting, a deer biologist, and a fanatical farmer. He is constantly experimenting and learning about the animal and its behaviors and patterns, and he plants appropriate, sustainable food plots to attract and hold deer on the reserve. Of course, Frank gives every aspect of his life full attention and passion, and he strives to do things the best way possible. This latest venture is no exception.

When asked how he learned all this, Frank says, "I googled it. Googled 'food plots.' Like everything else, someone else has to teach you. Read a book. Watch a video. Find it on Google."

Frank says taking care of 135 acres represents a lot of work. "The doctor told me that not too many guys like you, at eighty-six years of age, are doing what you're doing and are still alive. I told him that they're not lifting forty-pound sacks of fertilizer."

CHAPTER 24

— ❡ —

The Last Column

FRANK WRAPPED UP his columnist career at Plumbing & Mechanical Magazine with this, his final column. (Reprinted with permission from *PM Magazine*, 2004)

It's time to pass the torch to a new generation. For this month's column, I offer the following tips:

1. Avoid eating foods with a strong odor, such as garlic and onions, before heading into the woods.
2. Store your hunting clothes in unscented bags along with twigs, leaves, grasses, or deer-scent wafers. Do not use hunting clothes for changing oil or other household chores that might fill them with human scent.
3. Bow and arrow hunters, practice your archery while wearing your hunting clothes and gear.
4. Use a tightly sealed urine bottle for nature's call.
5. Twigs and branches could deflect an arrow. Double-check your shooting lanes.
6. Big bucks tend to be nocturnal in season. Your best chance to get one is very early or very late in the day.

Oh, wait. I forgot. This article is supposed to be about Business Tips. It's become increasingly easy for me to overlook that during deer-hunting season, when this is being written.

Not that I don't have other important pursuits during the off-season. There's plenty of fishing to catch up on, for example, plus my sorely neglected golf game. I'm embarrassed to tell you how many handicap strokes I carry these days thanks to my screwed-up priorities.

The Business of Contracting

My top priority for the last four decades has been business. First, it had to do with founding and operating Blau Plumbing & Heating. For the last decade or so, I've turned more and more of it over to my capable sons Jimmy and Bobby, but I still had business on the brain. During much of the 1990s, I was consumed with Contractors 2000, which I cofounded in 1992 and helped shepherd into the industry's finest organization for PHC service contractors.

I also found myself on the road much of the time, teaching "The Business of Contracting" to thousands of PHC contractors throughout the country. Also, since 1987, I've contributed this column of the same name to *Plumbing & Mechanical* magazine.

It seems like almost yesterday when that started. The financial end of contracting was a subject nobody else seemed to be addressing at the time. Most articles in the trade magazines focused on plumbing issues, with some attention given to marketing. However, it's always been my contention that you can be the most talented plumber in the world as well as the world's best marketer, but you will still fall flat on your face as a plumbing contractor if you don't have a handle on the financial end of the business.

Unfortunately, more than 90 percent of the contractors in our industry don't have the knowledge and/or will to crunch the numbers in a way that results in adequate compensation for themselves and their faithful, hardworking employees, and a healthy bottom line. This was true in 1987 and remains true today. It will remain true for all eternity until this industry changes its way of thinking about itself.

Through my column in *PM* and seminars, I have reached tens of thousands of plumbing contractors with a twofold message: (1) they are far more important contributors to our society than they give themselves credit for, and (2) they and their employees ought to be rewarded far more than they are.

Nothing in my professional life has been more gratifying than to have been an instrument of change for the better in the lives of hundreds of contractors and thousands of their employees throughout the industry. I'm referring to the contractors from coast to coast who have "taken the medicine" and revamped their business practices to get the selling prices they need to succeed in business and to leave a legacy to their families, employees, and communities at large. This has led to numerous friendships so powerful that I've neglected the deer, fish, and birdies.

Easing into Retirement

In last month's column, I wrote about "The Four Legs of Financial Security," pertaining to retirement. This is something most contractors haven't planned for and can't afford. So too many of them keep working long beyond the time when they should be expected to.

It's time to practice what I preach. Many years ago I began planning for my retirement and built up a considerable nest egg to draw from. Well, it's finally dawned on me that it's time to start doing that.

Last year I bought 135 acres of prime wooded land in northern Wisconsin. Since then I've spent most of my time there, constructing a building, creating two and a half miles of nine-foot-wide trails within the boundary lines of the property, and indulging in my passions for hunting and fishing. On the twenty-third of this month, I'll turn seventy-four, and that's what I intend to spend more of my time doing for however much time the Good Lord decides to grant me.

So this will be my last regular article for *PM*. My good friends at *PM* have informed me that they will publish any articles I wish to contribute from now on, and I may take them up on their gracious offer now and then. However, from now on, my successor will author each monthly edition of Business Tips.

Thinking Alike

Though I am departing from the scene, the industry at large is no less in need of someone to keep reminding them to crunch those numbers and instructing them on how to do it. Several months ago I addressed this issue with my good friend Jim Olsztynski. I asked him whether he had given any thought to a possible successor. Turns out he had. And without any previous discussion or prompting by me, he mentioned the same person I had in mind.

That's Randy Hilton. Randy is a former owner of a plumbing service firm, whom I met in the early 1990s as a fellow member of Contractors 2000. He has since sold his business and works as a consultant, with Contractors 2000 included among his clients. You'll find Randy as a source of wisdom when it comes to contractor finances, marketing, and other operational areas. I look forward to reading his articles.

I'm told *PM* will keep the name Business Tips as the title of Randy's column, partly as a way to keep my legacy alive. I appreciate that consideration.

I'm not going to entirely fade away. You'll still be able to reach me at my office from time to time and maybe at Contractors 2000 meetings now and then. But it's time to pass the torch to a worthy successor and to make those deer and fish earn their living.

I'll close with one more piece of advice. I've mentioned neglecting my beloved pastimes in what should have been my retirement years. Even more deeply, I regret devoting so much time to traveling around this country from one end to the other, presenting my seminars, that I've missed out on so many events in the lives of my nine children and nineteen grandchildren. Unlike outdoor sports, catching up on these activities is impossible. They are gone forever.

Don't let these events pass you by. Make time to attend your kids' ball games, school plays, and whatever other activities they may participate in. Once they grow up, it's too late to make up for lost time.

God bless, and thank you for your support and friendship.

(Reprinted with permission from *PM Magazine*, 2004)

It's no surprise that after Frank announced he would no longer be writing a column for *PM*, plenty of readers sent us their thoughts on his retirement.

Dear Frank,

It was with mixed emotions that we read about your retirement in this month's issue of *PM*. While we are very happy that you will finally get some much-deserved relaxation, we are saddened by the gap that your retirement will cause in this industry. We are sure that Randall Hilton will do an excellent job of filling the void you leave behind.

A few years ago, our business was the kind that you so often write about. We were a steadfast time-and-material shop, and we were clueless regarding our true cost of doing business. In fact, my husband, David, and I were so dead set against flat rate pricing that he occasionally "pushed your buttons" and often commented that "those kind of rates will never fly in our small market."

You, among others, finally convinced us to crunch our numbers because we couldn't possibly run a decent business at the rates we were charging. How right you were, Frank. What a shock it was to us to find that we were losing money consistently on every job. Once we knew our costs, flat rate pricing was soon to follow.

When we changed our way of doing business, it opened up a whole new world for us. We have increased not only our profits and our customer satisfaction, but we have expanded our services as well. Instead of living a miserable day-to-day existence that included unhappy customers and even unhappier business owners, we actually look forward to working on our business.

All the money in the world could never repay you for the sound advice you gave us.

Maureen K. Francis
David G. Francis Plumbing & Heating
Norwich, NY

Dear Frank,

I wanted to wish you the best and also thank you for all you have done not only for the industry but for me personally. When I met you in 1997, I was struggling and didn't have a clue what to do. I had been in business since 1981 and had gotten an associate's degree in business in the

1980s by attending night school. Still, I wasn't equipped to be running a contracting business.

I had been caught up in the "going rate" mentality and was fast going broke. I really think my meeting you was providential. Since I attended your seminar, I have completely turned my business around. Instead of operating on what Randy Hilton calls the "cost minus 10 percent," I now base my prices on what it takes to give my customers the service they deserve, while paying myself and my crew what we deserve.

Thanks again. At that time I never dreamed I could be knocking down a six-figure income and paying all my bills, let alone being involved in charitable activities. I'm really enjoying life these days.

Dusty S. Cook
Dynamic Plumbing
Houston, TX

A special thanks to Frank Blau for his contributions over the years to both the industry and *PM*. This man has given a good kick in the pants to those who would listen. And to those who listened and learned, they usually started to understand the difference between cash flow and net profit. I'm grateful for his herculean efforts to teach business to contractors and will miss his presence in the magazine. Thanks, Frank, for your friendship and tutorials.

Paul Pollets
Advanced Radiant Technology
Seattle, WA

Let me chime in here with how much Uncle Frank has helped me and others in this trade. He has been a champion for all sectors of our industry for years. I first saw him back in 1988 at a PHCC-sponsored seminar, and I knew he was the real deal. No nonsense; no bullshit; no touchy feely; no "woulda, coulda, shoulda"—just plain old-fashioned, in-your-face common sense.

If you didn't like it, tough. If you wanted to make excuses about how you couldn't possibly charge as much as he was talking about, he said, "Fine, don't change but quit wasting my time here."

At first I was a little put off by Frank's gruffness, but I knew in my heart the only thing that would work for me and the others that day was total honesty in dealing with the numbers that Frank was showing us. So I watched, and I listened to someone who really knew how business is supposed to work.

It was like watching an artist paint. He started out at nine o'clock in the morning with a blank canvas and ended up at four o'clock in the afternoon with a masterpiece. Only a fool couldn't see he was right; only a fool wouldn't change; only a fool wouldn't go home and do the things that needed to be done to help his or her family and business. But sadly that day there were many fools in that class, and some of them failed to act. A few of them have finally made the changes and are still around, but many of them didn't and are gone.

I have had many conversations with Frank since then, and he has always taken the time to share some of his knowledge with me, whether it be about the industry or life itself. What a joy it is to talk with someone who really cares about you as a person and wants to sincerely help you make your life better. And that in a nutshell is what Uncle Frank has always done best.

Gene Burch
Gene Burch Plumbing Heating & Air
Novato, CA

My longtime friend, Frank Blau, is going fishing and hunting? This is unbelievable! What about all the contractors who still don't see the light, who still need to be converted into progressive businesspeople? What a gap his departure will leave.

Frank has been an institution to this industry. No one can compare to his unselfish commitment and dedication to help anyone seeking his advice. He has brought peace and wealth to many contractors with his unbridled energy and unyielding will to lift this industry from the doldrums of doom. Frank is a true industry pioneer who has taken many arrows in the back. He can now go out to the wild blue yonder and revolutionize hunting and fishing. Thanks, Frank, for all the education.

Chuck Sternod
The Dwyer Group
Waco, TX

My two sons, Matt and Jeremy, and I met Frank at a business class he put on in Cleveland in the spring of 2000. His class has made a difference in our lives as nothing else has. It is with great appreciation, respect, and admiration that we wish Frank all God's blessings and a long and enjoyable retirement.

He has an extended family he has educated and mentored who will go on forever. All the time and effort he has given our industry are appreciated more than you will ever know.

God bless you, Frank, and all of your family. Enjoy your retirement and know that you weren't one of the herd. You stood out, took measure of what needed to be done, and completed the job as any good plumber would do.

James C. Mills
Precision Plumbing and Welding
Lancaster, OH

Dear Frank,

I want to wish you a happy and well-deserved retirement. You have had a great impact on me and my business as well as on many others in our great industry. I first attended one of your seminars in 1994 and then another in 1996.

You and your sons allowed me to come visit you in 1997 and spend the better part of the day. We used your services for our flat rate book for several years (we now do our own). Although we still do some new construction for favored clients, we have moved into the service area more each year. I always considered you as a mentor. You treated me as a friend. I will always be thankful for that.

Again, I wish you the best. May God bless you.
Russ Wegner
Wegner Plumbing Company
Mokena, IL

Dear Frank,

Congratulations on your upcoming retirement. I agree with you. It is time. You don't want to die in the saddle. Grab some years while the body still functions. I sold my plumbing and heating business in 1994, at age fifty-four, and came to Florida for some of the good life.

I just read where an entrepreneur said life is lived in three parts: learning, earning, and serving. You pretty well covered the bases. I think you did a fantastic job at educating and trying to educate the shop owners across this great nation. Some listened and prospered...I will leave the others alone.

Your advice was usually given with a salty flair. And that is OK. Tends to make people listen closer. I didn't always agree with your philosophy, such as flat rate. I don't think that there is a "one size fits all" when it comes to business. But that isn't what this note is about.

This note is to say thank you for a job well done. You didn't preach in vain. You're one of the "old warriors" who earned his place in the sun. Enjoy your time, and God bless you.
Chuck Garot
Naples, FL

I took one of Frank's seminars back in 1992. Wow, what an eye-opener. He inspired me to give it a try right from the start by using his business strategies and going into business for myself. My wife had a big part, too. In January 1993 she earned a great promotion at her job and said if I had any inkling of going out on my own, now was the time.

So with $300 in the bank and two small jobs lined up, I gave my employer notice. Did I mention I did this sixteen months after getting married and buying a house?

Well, skip to today. We are now an LLC with three full-time mechanics and a part-time office/bookkeeper (no, not my wife). My wife left her job in 1996 to raise our three daughters: six, four, and twenty-one months. I am most proud of the fact that I have been able to give her that choice.

We provide three weeks' vacation, paid holidays, health benefits, a retirement plan, and uniforms. My only confession is that I still haven't completely made the jump to all set pricing. We mix set pricing with some Time &Material pricing. I am sorry, but this seems to work for us.

I just wanted to say thanks to Frank for all he's done for this industry, and if it were up to me, the licensing process would have to include your seminar.

William R. Gripp
Gripp Plumbing & Heating, LLC
Parsippany, NJ

Dear Mr. Blau,

We've never met, but when I read your last regular column, I felt compelled to thank you for all the free advice. I haven't been in the plumbing business for several years but am in the service business contracting to industries in our area.

I have continued to read *Plumbing & Mechanical* just for the management articles and found your advice sound and perfectly matched for our business, as service is also our main commodity.

I read several business magazines each month, but none address the meat and potatoes of business as well as you do. Your articles are right on the money. So, thanks again for all the good advice, and I wish you luck with the hunting and fishing.

R. Scott Gibbs
R. D. Gibbs Ent. Inc.
Bloomfield, MO

CHAPTER 25

— ❧ —

Influencing an Industry

Frank Blau: The Most Influential Contractor of the Last Twenty-Five Years

A Complex, Controversial Man on a Mission Who's Helped Thousands of Contractors

By Jim Olsztynski

A moment stands out in memory that speaks volumes to endorse our tribute to Frank Blau as *PM's* "Most Influential Contractor." It was at a "Super Meeting" of Contractors 2000 (now Nexstar) held in New Orleans in fall of 1997. At the closing banquet, President Brad Martin presented Blau with a customary plaque upon conclusion of his two-year term on the board of directors. Then, speaking to an audience of more than three hundred people, Martin invited everyone among them whom Frank Blau had personally helped to come toward the podium. Virtually every seat emptied as contractors surged forward and surrounded the stage. Then a spontaneous, thunderous, and sustained ovation arose, the likes of which this reporter had never before witnessed at any business event.

That audience represented only a small fraction of the service contractors Frank has helped over the years. Their numbers certainly stand in the thousands.

By "helped," I don't mean in a casual way. The Business of Contracting articles Frank wrote for this magazine for almost two decades were indeed helpful to thousands upon thousands of readers, but that's just the tip of the iceberg.

Reading Tiger Woods's tips in *Golf Digest* might well help improve your game a bit, but it doesn't compare to how good you could become if you had the great fortune to receive a bunch of extended personal lessons from him. Frank Blau has given that kind of hands-on attention to myriad contractors over the years.

For years he hit the road, conducting paid seminars that usually ended up around the break-even mark once all expenses were tallied. Beyond that, he has spent countless unpaid hours chatting on the phone with contractors from near and far. Many of them have made a pilgrimage to visit Blau Plumbing & Heating in Milwaukee to see details of an operation that ranks as one of the most successful PHC service companies in the country—again, without charge. (Frank retired from the business several years ago, and two of his nine children, sons Jim and Bob Blau, now run it.)

Frank doesn't believe in business secrets. He's always been willing to share operational best practices, even with direct competitors. His abiding philosophy is that a rising tide raises all ships. To him the biggest competitive threat is not from companies that operate like his at the upper rungs of professionalism—and charge for their services accordingly. Instead, he sees the entire industry dragged down by hordes of contractors, who may be technically astute but clueless about running a business,. Frank spent the first half of his career making himself and his family financially secure. He's spent the last half as a man on a mission, helping fellow service contractors realize the same kind of prosperity.

A crowning achievement of Frank's career was the formation of Contractors 2000/Nexstar, of which he was the driving force. Almost a thousand firms have been members since the affinity group was formed in 1992, and they have been privy to some of the best business and marketing information available to service companies in this or any other industry. Most of those members, past and present, would tell you that crossing paths with Frank Blau was one of the best things that ever happened in their lives.

Customers Get What They Pay For: Frank is one of the industry's pioneers of flat rate pricing for residential service work. He has been controversial in that role because it's common knowledge that flat rating is a method to disguise high labor rates that otherwise would cause customers to gasp if broken out in a time and materials format. This brings charges of gouging by folks who tend to overlook the flip side of this coin. Frank Blau has always preached top-notch customer service and high employee compensation along with elevated prices. He's also been generous, donating to industry, community, and charitable causes.

One of the things that always impressed me about Blau Plumbing & Heating was that a vast majority of the company's business came from repeat customers. Gougers can get away with fleecing someone once, but when people keep coming back for more, you have to conclude they perceive value in the services rendered at the prices charged.

As important as all the expertise he's passed along is, there has been the boost Frank has given to the industry's self-esteem. No evangelist has ever preached with more fervor than he has, gospel centered around the message that PHC technicians and contractors bring valuable skills and services to society and deserve to be compensated accordingly. Smoke comes out of his ears at any notion that there ought to be limits to how much money a plumber or owner should make.

Curious Charisma: Years ago Frank coined the term *slugs* to refer to business-challenged contractors he contends are responsible for the industry's poor image. During the years he wrote for this magazine, I had a running battle with Frank over use of the term, which I felt—still do— was uncharitable and needlessly alienated many contractors who might otherwise be more receptive to his message. But getting Frank to change his ways is like trying to command the wind to stop howling. We agreed to disagree about this issue, and it points to an aspect of what I term his curious charisma.

Charisma is one of those words that is hard to define, but you know it when you see it. It's a rare trait of personal magnetism and persuasiveness, and Frank's version is curious because charisma is usually associated with charming personalities. Although I count myself among his close friends and admirers, neither I nor most of the thousands of other people who are members of this club would associate the word *charming* with Frank Blau. He can be blunt and profane to the point of insulting, and he is about as un-PC in his political and social views as one is likely to find in modern mainstream society. Many people with thin skins can't stand Frank Blau.

Yet this all translates into that curious charisma for the vast majority of us who know him. When Frank walks into a room, the center of gravity shifts in his direction. His charisma stems not as much from personality as from the power of his ideas and wisdom, and his generosity in sharing them.

Frank's outspokenness obscures perhaps the most pronounced characteristic that has contributed to his success. I've observed him in hundreds of settings spanning large meetings, small groups, and one-on-one conversations. The thing that strikes me most from all these interactions is that Frank is one of the best listeners I've ever known. It's said that the best salesmen talk only 10 percent of the time, and in most encounters with Frank, that's about where his voice ends up. He listens intently to what others have to say, and when he does finally speak up, it's clear he has absorbed the wheat and discarded the chaff.

Lasting Legacy: Soon to hit eighty, Frank Blau still maintains an office at his old company but spends much of his time tooling around at a rustic wildlife preserve he owns in Wisconsin. But he's still quite active in giving business advice to old and new friends, and he serves as honorary chairman of the Nexstar Legacy Foundation, whose scholarship program is named after him.

During these past twenty-five years, I've encountered a few other contractors who have been just as smart and successful as Frank Blau. But in terms of being influential, of touching other people's lives in a positive way, he vaults to the top of the list.

CHAPTER 26

Forever Mentoring

THE FRANK J. Blau Jr. Training Center, a 6,891-square-foot facility complete with state-of-the-art video and e-learning studio, training rooms, and meeting space, was dedicated on December 3, 2014.

In addition to the center, now located in a beautiful newer office building in St. Paul, Minnesota, there is an additional 6,653 square feet available for expansion.

At the center's grand opening ceremony, Nexstar president and CEO Jack Tester said, "Frank's mission for starting Nexstar, and what we carry on today, was to help contractors see the value of the services we provide for our communities. As an industry, we need to shore up our self-esteem and charge the right price to ensure we operate successful businesses, providing superior service to our customers and good jobs and benefits for those we employ."

A reunion of Nexstar executives: Current Nexstar CEO Jack Tester (standing) and former executives (left to right) Marla Coffin, Frank J. Blau Jr., and Greg Niemi. Photo courtesy of Kelly Faloon, *Plumbing & Mechanical.*

CHAPTER 27

∞

The FJB Effect

THERE IS NO denying the incredible, wide-reaching positive impact Frank and his potent "medicine" have had on thousands of students. Here are the stories of just a few.

Empowering Expectations by Jack Tester

It was late 1992. I was having a drink with Frank Blau right after I was hired to help get his new organization—Contractors 2000—off the ground. Frank was telling me—a green thirty-year-old aspiring executive—his views on management, delegation, hiring, motivation, and people development. I was on the edge of my seat, listening. Forty years of business experience was being shared with me for the price of a brandy Old Fashion.

I was feeling important and privileged. I must be pretty good for a man of Frank's stature to trust me with the fate of his dream organization. In moments like this, it is easy to get cocky, prideful, and a little too full of yourself. At that moment, that pretty much described me.

Right after Frank's management discussion, he got quiet and leaned a bit closer to me. His bling was gleaming. A gold eagle—life size almost—hung from his necklace. It was one of three gold chains swinging toward me in that moment.

As he got closer, his unblinking eyes became huge—partly for emphasis, mostly due to the magnification of his thick glasses. They looked about six inches around.

I expected to hear something profound. One more pearl of wisdom was about to drop. Maybe he was going to compliment me.

He said, "Jack, I love you and trust you to do a good job. But if you make a stupid mistake, *your ass is grass, and I'm the lawn mower.*" I gulped, terrified. I knew Frank was entrusting me with a very important mission, and he was very clear on what I needed to do to succeed *and* what would happen if I screwed it up.

There you have it. That is Frank in a nutshell. He trusts. He coaches. He does everything in his power to help you succeed. But he doesn't suffer fools. He is intolerant of lazy, stupid mistakes. He gives you a pass when you try mightily and fall short. He then helps you learn from the experience in a direct and supportive way. But if you don't try or make the same stupid mistake twice,…he fires up the lawn mower.

Not wanting to let Frank down drove me to be better. I thank Frank for all the time he spent with me, giving me his counsel and support. I'm also the better for the well-intended fear he put in my heart.

Lessons Learned from Frank Blau, by Al Levi

Sitting in a bar many years ago with Frank Blau, an industry giant, at a convention (trust me, it was all about the education), we got to talking about extended hour service.

Frank shared with me that 40 percent of his profitability came from his company's ability to better handle the after-hour calls than his competition. That was an eye-opener. But it was nothing new to me. I had been born into a family business that actively practiced the 24/7/365 philosophy by manning our own phones and having staff in the field to do just that. That said, Frank is king when it comes to numbers, and I had never sat back to realize just how right he was…until then.

Catching up with Frank at another meeting along the way, I made the mistake of complaining to Frank, "It's not fair that when a tech quits, I don't get all my stuff back."

Frank said, "The customer pays for it."

So I went on with my rant. "But, that's not fair!"

To which, Frank replied, "What don't you get? The customer pays for everything!"

I shut up and finally got the message.

I applied that learning experience at the bar those many years ago with Frank with a client of mine who asked me, "You mentioned that every fall and spring your company rerolled out the heating or cooling chapters of the manuals as a refresher and did other stuff to get the techs ready for the change of season. I would also like to do this, but who should pay for this type of training?"

So I replied as Frank had taught me to with, "Great question on who pays! This type of training—our company paid for all company training time. Ultimately, I was taught by Frank Blau that the customer pays for everything. And that approach only makes sense because all the things we do, from training, trucks, communication, and more, are in the customer's best interest. That's why training costs were part of our budget."

A couple of years later, Frank and I were at a different convention and found ourselves talking about business. Yes, it was a different bar.

We got to talking about the fallacy that computers can fix stupid practices in real-world accounting. Once again, I was in class because the great Frank Blau had told me, "If you can't run your company with a pad and a pencil, the computer will just obscure the facts."

Frank was and is a true innovator. He changed the way we approach the work we do and instilled pride in contractors that what they do is valuable to our society. And for that we're entitled to make a good wage and have the benefits we deserve for our hard work. We also owe it to our customers to charge enough so we can serve them the way they want and need to be served. Charging the right price is always in the customer's best interest.

The Gift of Time by Bill Raymond

There are many things that come to mind when I think of Frank Blau Jr. But through them all I'd be willing to bet that most come back to Frank's willingness, passion, and desire to give the gift of his time.

I first met Frank in 1995 when I mustered the courage to call him on the phone. I was a struggling contractor, working crazy hours, and nearly everyone in my company made more money than I. I was a faithful reader of Frank's Business of Contracting article in *Plumbing & Mechanical* magazine and was in search of a better way.

I called Frank; he answered and spent close to ninety minutes on the phone—teaching me, explaining to me, scolding me, and encouraging me. Ninety minutes with a perfect stranger.

The following year, I met Frank in person at an open house in Chicago for Nexstar Network (then Contractors 2000). This time I was one of thirty people spending a day with Frank. He spoke to every one of us throughout the day as if we were one of his children, convincing us that there is a better way and that contractors can and deserve to run a profitable business that provides for the owners, employees, and customers. Keep in mind that he had a business of his own at home, but he spent one full day with perfect strangers.

For the last nineteen years, I have watched Frank give the gift of his time. At trade shows or conferences, there is *always* someone around him willing to "take the medicine" and receive the gift of his time. He sits with individuals who hang on his every word. He stands with a group around him, listening to every word—people like me, looking for a better way.

I have heard every lesson and story Frank has to tell multiple times: how to determine a correct selling price, knowing your cost of doing business, the difference between markup and margin, the meaning of "70½," the lawn mower story, the fishing story, and so many more. I can never hear them enough. His gift has impacted the lives of thousands in a positive and profound way. My business and my life have been changed forever.

Perhaps his greatest lesson for all of us is to do the same. Give the gift of *your* time to impact the lives of others in a positive and profound way.

Peak Experiences by Bryan Schroll

There are certain monumental events in life, and I remember where I was when they happened: the 9/11 terrorist attacks, the first landing on the moon, and meeting Frank Blau.

I met Frank in January of 1993 at the first Contractors 2000/Nexstar meeting in Anaheim, California; I remember it like it was yesterday. The meetings had just concluded, and my brother and I were sitting at the bar, still making notes from the meetings, when Frank came up to us, put his arms around us, and asked, "So what do you guys think?" wondering what our opinion was about the meeting. We were already blown away with the ideas we'd acquired and things we had learned. Frank pulled up a stool and proceeded to open up his briefcase and share more of his golden nuggets of wisdom. "These are valve tags. This is a lifetime control warranty." He kept reaching in that briefcase for probably an hour. Before leaving that day, he said, "Your office is only eighty miles from Milwaukee. You should come up and see how we do things at Blau Plumbing."

Within a few weeks of returning from Anaheim, I got a phone call from Frank. "Bryan. What are you doing? Get your ass up here to Milwaukee!" I went up very early the next day. He spent the whole day with me, sharing everything from financial statements to truck inventory; he even took me out to the Dumpster to point out the Blau Plumbing stickers on the old water heaters. Then we were off to the kitchen and bath showroom and Making Waves hair salons.

I had read Frank's articles for years in *Plumbing & Mechanical* magazine, and I knew he was a very successful contractor. I found it really remarkable that this man was taking a genuine interest in my success by sharing both his knowledge and time. He had no personal agenda; he wasn't selling anything. He just wanted to help me.

Frank followed up every so often to make sure we "were taking the medicine." When he called the office, the receptionist asked who was calling. Frank jokingly responded, "Tell Bryan God is on the phone." The education, mentoring, and love from Frank Blau have been a godsend.

They have been life changing for me, my family, and our employees. I'm proud to be a Blau disciple.

We had joined C-2000/Nexstar expecting to get a few good ideas to improve our business; we came away with information that would change the way we did business forever, and we had an incredible friend and mentor in Frank Blau.

Second Father by Dan Weltman

In January 1992, during the height of the Gulf War recession, a supplier insisted I attend the Frank J. Blau "Business of Contracting" seminar, being held locally. As a business-ignorant person, I knew I needed help in paying the bills, let alone myself.

Long story short, I walked in and saw a middle-aged gentleman sporting hearing aids, wearing trifocal glasses, and puffing one Marlboro after another. A few minutes into the seminar, I was mesmerized by such terms, then foreign to me, as "billable hour overhead" and "gross margin." I took everything in. I went home and couldn't sleep that night.

The very next day, I tore through my checkbook and receipts. I discovered that changes were needed in my small company. So change we did.

In a short time, business started turning around. Frank's preaching worked so well that I wrote him a letter, then another and another. We were beginning to prosper in the midst of a recession.

Finally the phone call came from Frank: "You should come to Milwaukee this August. A group of progressive contractors are meeting in my business to start a college of knowledge. We are thinking of calling the new organization Contractors 2000."

So I booked my flight to Milwaukee, and many industry giants surrounded me; time came to choose the founding board of directors, and Frank nominated me. Contractors 2000, now Nexstar, has created new avenues of education and friendships I never imagined possible.

I consider Frank a second father. We have become very close friends over the twenty-one-plus years since that winter day in 1992. He was, and continues to be, my role model in business and life. I still consult Frank on business challenges, and he's always there for me.

Frank preached profits and prosperity over two decades ago, and his passion burns as bright as ever.

Thank you, Frankie Jr., for all you've done for me, my family, my employees, and this great industry.

Lunch and Life by Dave Vogelgesang

Dear Frank,

My dad, Hank, and I first met you in 1992 at your "Business of Contracting" seminar in Minneapolis. At that time his plumbing business was deeply in the red, but he'd heard that your "flat rate" method of pricing could help business. He decided to attend and asked whether I would like to come along.

I remember sitting through the morning session, totally bored, and thinking what a bunch of BS you were shoveling. Flat rate will not work with our customers and so forth. (I know you've heard all the excuses.) I thought I had my dad convinced to leave the seminar at the lunch break, but we decided to at least eat lunch with the group before leaving.

After lunch he decided to check the first part of the afternoon session. I remember being pissed off that I would have to sit through more of this crap, and I couldn't leave—he drove the truck.

I don't remember specifically what changed my mind during the afternoon session, but I do remember that we thought "flat rate" was worth a shot. At that time we were 120 days out with almost every wholesaler, and our accounts receivable was ridiculously high, but at least our doors were still open.

To make a long story short, we ended up visiting your business, used your price book, and started flat rate in June of 1992. Aqua City is now a healthy company that, with continued success, will grow for many more years.

Frank, I know this letter is *long* past due. I've told myself many times to sit down and write a thank-you letter to you, but I just never have done it. You and I have talked only a couple of times, and you know I am on the "quiet side," so, unfortunately, it takes a while for me to get around to letters like this.

I often wonder how different my life would be if my dad and I hadn't met you. Our business is successful in large part due to what you have taught us and the industry as a whole. If we hadn't tried flat rate pricing or joined Contractors 2000, I know my life would be very different.

I wouldn't have met the many wonderful friends from C2000. I doubt that I could afford the home I'm living in now. And given the way I was living my life previous to 1992, I very seriously doubt I would have my beautiful daughter.

I've been thinking about you quite a lot over the past year, Frank. What would I be doing if I hadn't attended that one seminar? What would have happened if Dad and I had left the seminar before lunch like I wanted? I think about that lunch at every C2000 super meeting and every peer group meeting.

Frank, I don't know what else to say, so I'll just say thank you. Thank you for that lunch.

Love you, Frank.
Dave Vogelgesang
Aqua City Plumbing

One of a Kind by Julie Wieman

I first heard about Frank Blau back in 1992 when my dad, John MacGregor, told me he was joining an organization I'd never heard of before.

He said Frank was starting it, so he was sending a check, because he believed in what Frank taught and was willing to support his venture. Our company joined C2000 in December of 1992. Here we are, over twenty-one years later, and there is hardly a Nexstar program I haven't implemented into my company, thanks to Frank's vision.

I consider him to be one of my dearest friends and greatest mentors. I have never seen the man hesitate to question people about whether they are saving for retirement, charging the right price, providing for their employees, building their costs into their price with a healthy profit, or telling those who are in need of a proctologist.

Frank continues to bless us with his stories and experience at annual Nexstar events, and he can always be seen holding court throughout the weekends. Frank is one of a kind when it comes to human beings who selflessly give of themselves for the betterment of others.

I wish him all the happiness and health in the world, while he continues to work on growing big deer, and I look forward to many, many more lobby chats with him in the future. I love you, Frank! "Thank you" just doesn't seem like enough to say.

Julie Wieman

President, MacGregor Plumbing and Heating Inc.

Harbor Springs, MI

It Works by Kenny Chapman

I first met Frank in 1996 at the Pumper and Cleaner Expo in Long Beach, California. My little drain-cleaning business was only two years old, and this was my first industry-specific trade show, complete with educational breakouts and everything. I was excited beyond belief.

Since I couldn't afford airfare or the conference hotel, I took a road trip from Colorado and was staying at a seedy off-brand hotel miles from the convention center. I didn't care, though, because pinching pennies was the only life I knew to this point. I didn't understand how to realize my potential at this stage in my life.

The first morning I ate an early breakfast at the conference hotel, eager to have some success rub off on me. After breakfast and a good walk around the show floor, it became time for the educational breakout sessions.

I knew that I wanted to learn about the latest tools and equipment, but there was also a seminar that sounded intriguing. I decided to attend Frank's workshop, "The Business of Contracting."

The session was incredibly informative, and I thought my head was going to explode in the first hour. I thought I knew simple math, yet I couldn't understand margin versus markup. I struggled with the content, because I didn't understand the numbers. I struggled with the overhead pricing sheet, because I didn't believe it could cost that much to run a business. I struggled with flat rate pricing, because I thought nobody would pay those prices.

When it came time for questions, I was quick to raise my hand. Frank said, "Yes, what is it, young man?" I replied with a very convincing dissertation, addressing how I understood that his concepts worked in the city, but I lived in small-town America, and *it just wouldn't work in my market.*

In one of the calmest voices I've ever heard Frank speak, he waved his hand in my direction and said, "Young man, please stand up." I was a bit nervous, but I slowly rose to my feet. As soon as I was standing, he pointed his finger at me and loudly proclaimed, "Ladies and gentlemen, this is what a maggot in our industry looks like!"

The room erupted in laughter. I was in shock. I couldn't believe what had just happened. The room went to break, and I left the workshop thinking how crazy this old man was. It was a long five years later before I finally gave Frank's teachings the real test and "took the medicine" myself. This decision to implement Frank's philosophies improved my business and life forever.

I feel incredibly blessed that Frank has embraced me as a disciple of his to continue his message. The day he told me to carry his message in my own way is one of the most special days of my life. I'm honored to be part of this book and will be forever grateful for what Frank has taught me. Thank you, Frank.

Helping First by Michael Bohinc

I first met Frank back in the 1980s through the pages of *Plumbing & Mechanical* magazine. It was a chance meeting. I wanted to learn more about my father's profession, so I leafed through the magazine. Most articles and columns may as well have been written in Mandarin Chinese, because I didn't understand them at all.

One, however, caught my attention because it had the word *business* in its title. That column, The Business of Contracting, was written in my language, the language of business. I was thrilled to see that someone was writing about and focusing on the *business* side of the industry.

In 1989, I went to my first "Business of Contracting" seminar. I got my dad to come to the seminar with me. I had been trying to get him to increase his billing rates, because he was losing money. His salary, like many others, was whatever was left after paying everyone else. Sometimes there wasn't *anything* left.

Dad and Frank had a frank conversation (pardon the pun). My dad's eyes started to open because he was hearing it from someone *besides* his son. My dad "took the medicine." It was at this point that things started to change.

Two years later, my dad booked Frank to do his "Business of Contracting" seminar at the Ohio PHCC Convention. That same year, we implemented flat rate pricing. Two years after that, my family's plumbing business joined Frank in Contractors 2000 (now Nexstar Network). We began to soar like the eagle Frank so dearly loves.

This is the best story I can share about Frank and one I believe defines the man. I had the pleasure of spending a few days with Frank at his deer farm with Randall Hilton and a couple of plumbing contractors. Early in the afternoon on Saturday, Frank's phone in the cabin rang. He answered it. The call was from a contractor who needed Frank's help. The rest of us were outside, enjoying the beautiful day.

After a while, we started to worry about Frank. We went back to the cabin and found Frank still on the phone with the contractor. Frank spent three and a half hours on the phone that afternoon helping that contractor. He got his own private "Business of Contracting" seminar. There was no invoice, no selling of books, videos, and so forth. He simply asked the contractor to "take the medicine" and commit to charging what he needed to make a respectable profit.

Outside of my father, Frank is the person who has impacted my career the most. In 2005, Frank was the first recipient of the distinguished Servant Leader Award from the Service Roundtable. I was blessed to be among the few who were there when he received it. In 2012, I was honored and humbled to receive the same award as my mentor. I am proud to be a Blau disciple. I am most proud to call him my dear friend.

Michael A. Bohinc, CPA

CFO, Norhio Plumbing Inc.

Owner, Keeping Score Inc.

Good Medicine by Tim McGuire

I met Frank in 1991 while attending one of his "Business of Contracting" seminars. He invited my parents and me to Milwaukee to visit his operation and see firsthand how a successful service operation was run. I reluctantly took him up on his offer, and away we went.

We were blown away, of course, and we could clearly see that we had met someone who was about to change the course of our lives.

After all the number crunching that was central to Frank's teaching was done, $83.50 was the number on the calculator. "What does that mean, Frank?" I asked.

He replied, "That's your breakeven,!" Frank, sensing my apprehension, said, "What's the matter?"

I stated that we were charging sixty-eight dollars per hour, and we were the most expensive contractor in town. Frank stated, "Congratulations. You're not losing as much as most of the slugs across the country."

Fortunately for us, we took the medicine, changed our pricing, and became students of the business, thus changing the course of our destiny. We were able to have a front-row seat as Contractors 2000 was formed and transformed to Nexstar Network.

Today I enjoy a successful company, my folks are retired, and I have been able to meet the financial and personal goals I set for myself.

One memory of Frank that will always stay with me is the time I shared a room with him at a Nexstar Legacy event in Scottsdale. I found out that Frank needs to sleep in a recliner due to chronic back pain. The problem was, this hotel didn't have recliners in the room. To solve the problem, Frank propped up some pillows on his bed and slept in the sitting position.

The next thing I remember was awakening to a scream of pain. I found Frank kneeling on the floor, unable to get up. It was quite a sight to behold—your mentor and friend in agony, kneeling in his Skivvies next to your bed.

What to do now? After several attempts to lift Frank up, I finally managed to get him into the desk chair. Frank slept the rest of the night in that chair and seemed quite fine in the morning.

The humility of that experience sort of sums up who Frank really is for me. Frank didn't teach for personal gain, save that of the satisfaction he received when another one of us ignorant contractors saw the light and changed our course.

Frank taught freely and without cost in order for others to be set free from the chains of their own ignorance.

Well done, good and faithful servant. Well done.

Tim McGuire

Minneapolis, MN

What's Cooking? by Marla Coffin

It was a very cold January in 1994 when I joined Contractors 2000. "Joining" for me wasn't as a member but as the second employee of Frank Blau's organization.

When I came on board, the only person I had met from Contractors 2000 was my boss, Jack Tester. We were preparing for a Super Meeting, and it was at this event that I would meet the founder, Frank Blau. Jack wanted me to be prepared for the moment and went into great detail, describing Frank and leaving me with an impression of a man who was larger than life.

It so happened that I "met" Frank sooner than expected. Upon answering the office phone one day, a gruff "Who is this?" greeted me. I quickly figured out it was Frank on the other end of the line. *Gulp!* Frank asked me, "What's cooking?" and I proceeded to explain to him my current projects. He listened for a bit, and then he repeated his question. "What's cooking?" Having no idea how to respond, I replied, "I don't know, Frank. What's cooking?"

Any anxiety I may have had from meeting Frank melted away upon hearing his response. "Chicken—ya wanna neck?"

That's the moment I fell in love with Frank, and to this day, "What's cooking?" is our special greeting.

Love you, Frank.

Marla Coffin

Former senior VP and general manager, Nexstar Network

Two-Father Daughter by Lisa Schardt

My "Dad," Frank Blau, and I go way back—to when I was born. You see, I was born and raised in Menomonee Falls, Wisconsin. Our homes were twelve miles apart.

I am a plumber's daughter; my dad worked for a Blau competitor. He was the hardest-working man I have ever known. A jar of GOOP was always on the kitchen sink, where he would spend fifteen minutes each day, trying to get that grunge off his skin. I have always respected this industry and the talent of many.

Blau Plumbing was a name I frequently heard or saw. I remember driving to our lake home and seeing the "Blau bathtub" on the tall pole right off the freeway. Whenever I made a comment about it, my dad (who was typically a very mild-mannered man) simply said, "He's a crook." When I asked why, I wouldn't get a response. This went on for years and years.

In 1982, my dad was laid off from the plumbing competitor. As sad as it was, the company eventually went out of business. My dad found his next career with Briggs & Stratton and recently retired.

In 2000, I went to work for Contractors 2000 (now Nexstar).

Shortly after I started, I had a conversation with my dad and tried to explain what I did—and who I was working with (Frank). I was proud that I was able to be in the same industry as my dad and was bragging a bit—until he said, "You are working for that crook?" *Ouch.*

Once I explained that Frank was the founder of this great company and what our goals were—to raise the bar in the industry—he settled down. Then I softly reminded him of which plumbing company was still in business and which one hadn't made it. *Double ouch.*

So like most American families, it's a subject we no longer discuss. It's swept nicely under the rug, where it will stay.

Of course, when I met Frank for the first time and explained my path to Contractors 2000, he immediately told me I was his "long-lost daughter," and we have been close ever since—hence the reason I call him Dad.

I have the honor and pleasure of selling memberships to the best organization in the world.

When I started in 2000, less than 15 percent of people I spoke to had ever heard of flat rate. Most were *priced under* fifty dollars per hour, Time & Material. Those were the toughest days. I did a rough breakeven with them on our call and end up at $180 to $200 per billable hour (another foreign concept). They couldn't argue—it was *their* numbers. And so it began...

Not a day goes by that I don't think of Frank and his wisdom. I speak of him often in the calls I have with prospective members. Too many of my calls are with "Slugs," and I feel it's my duty and responsibility to give them what I call a little "Frank love" and tell them to pull their heads out of their *&#. You know...Just fill in the blank.

So my real job is to keep Frank's message alive, to keep spreading the word, and sometimes to beat it into their heads. I must carry the Nexstar torch for him, and I do it with pride, respect, and admiration.

Changing the world…and changing lives, one Slug at a time, right, Dad? (Just don't make me tell the "70½ story"!)

Much love,

Lisa Schardt

Business enhancement coach

Nexstar Network Inc

Industry Icon, Rebel, Revolutionary, Plus a Sweetheart of a Man by Greg Niemi

Frank Blau committed his life to the betterment of lives and businesses as well as the entire industry of plumbing, heating, cooling, and electrical contractors. He has led by example.

His lifelong work has been to help independent business owners be better business owners—to be successful and respected owners plus to earn the good living they deserve to earn.

Whether you agree with all of Frank's views, he has changed an industry. Without a doubt he's improved the world we live in, and we all need to be thankful for this.

How do I know Frank? I had the distinct pleasure or—dare I say—pain to take over the helm of Contractors 2000 (now Nexstar), the training organization he and others had founded.

At the time the organization was in a dark place. C2000 was struggling, and this pained Frank and all of us who were part thereof. I can remember, as can he, the meeting we had in a hotel just up the street from the office. We had our work ahead of us.

It was after this meeting that I was selected to lead the organization out of this predicament. And I did. I was able, with the support of so many others, including Frank, to right the organization and put it back on track as the leader in our industry. This was a huge accomplishment we remain proud of.

Throughout that turnaround and my years thereafter, Frank treated me with great respect. I earned his respect, and he earned mine (time and time again). I knew I had to earn his respect with continued perfor-mance and could never, ever rely on past accomplishments. We had a marvelous run during our time, and I know we are both delighted by this.

Now I'm not going to say I didn't have a tinge of fear anytime he called, because I absolutely did. After all, I was managing "his baby." When he called, I thought, Oh boy, what is this going to be about? Which, of course, I quickly knew.*

Frank never hesitated to make his views and opinions absolutely crys-tal clear and leave the sugar coating off the table. Yet I can tell you his intentions were always genuine. He always left the final decisions and reins with me to lead our organization. Frank was an intimidating, empow-ering, and loving man all wrapped up in one.

I was also able to work with Frank and John Ward and others to found a nonprofit organization to give back to the industry the gift of education via scholarships. This is just another fine example of Frank's legacy, which will take care of many future generations to come.

I am forever grateful for the lessons he has taught me and am thankful for the impact he has made on the industry and my life personally. We are all better because of Frank Blau Jr.

We love you, Frank. OXO.

Greg A. Niemi

Former president & CEO, Nexstar Inc.

June 28, 1999–November 11, 2011

* I always knew it was a great call when it opened with Frank saying, "How is Gregory the Great doing?" I also quickly knew it may not be so great if he didn't open with that.

CHAPTER 28

—— ✧ ——

Servant Roundtable Award: Matt Michel

A SERVANT LEADER Leads by Example, Not Command, and Is Compelled to Help Others

(Editor's Note: The following is adapted from a speech Matt Michel, CEO of the Service Roundtable, gave during an awards ceremony in January 2005.)

Frank was struggling, swimming against the current of the cold, frigid waters of Lake Michigan. The teenager was cold. He was tired. He was scared. It would have been so easy to surrender, to give up, to let the storm swallow him. But it wasn't just his life at stake. The lives of others depended upon him. He had to keep going. His father and his friend were counting on him. They were behind him somewhere, clinging to an overturned boat, hanging on.

The storm had come up suddenly, swamping the small boat, losing the motor. Frank was the best swimmer of the three.

The seventeen-year-old was the only one who had a chance to make it to shore and find help. It wasn't much of a chance. He had to carve his way through a mile of water. He started to cramp, so he changed from a crawl to a backstroke. When he could no longer maintain the backstroke, he switched to a breaststroke and then to a crawl. Over and over, stroke after stroke, he kept moving. By now every movement was agony, but he drew comfort from the agony. The pain proved he was still alive. The pain seemed to hold the hypothermia at bay.

He couldn't see the shore. He swam by dead reckoning. It was a miracle that he swam straight. It was a miracle that he covered a mile in the turbulent, icy water. It was a miracle that he was found soon after he stumbled ashore, freezing to death. It was a miracle that he managed to hoarsely whisper the information about the others drifting on the water. It was a miracle that the coast guard found them.

The next day, the local papers told the tale of the "seventeen-year-old hero" who beat the odds to save his father and his friend. And Frank Blau has been miraculously saving people ever since.

Frank saved countless others through his life. He may not have saved them as dramatically as that nearly fatal day on Lake Michigan, but he saved them nonetheless. He saved them from themselves. He saved them from the poverty of their ignorance.

Frank Blau was a union plumber. He persevered through a low-wage apprenticeship to become a journeyman. Then with $500, he launched Blau Plumbing. With his brother as business partner, Frank built Blau Plumbing into one of the largest new construction plumbing companies in the country. He built a showroom and convinced builders to send people to the showroom where Frank sold upgrades, increasing the profitability of his company and of the builders he worked with.

The showroom was an innovation in its day, one of many. Many business practices that people take for granted today were unusual at best and often controversial when Frank Blau first tried them. For example, Frank was one of the first to see the lucrative potential of the service business, and he changed the direction of his company to pursue it. As a service business, Blau Plumbing became smaller but also more profitable.

Frank coined the unique selling proposition (USP) of "sudden service." He hired professionals to work on a logo and tested different logo concepts. To take advantage of the space fever gripping the nation during the Kennedy administration, Frank and his brother settled on a spaceman in a bathtub with a helicopter rotor. Both the logo and the USP have been imitated.

When every other plumber merely listed his company in the Yellow Pages, Frank saw the opportunity presented by a large Yellow Pages display ad and took advantage of it. He purchased large panel trucks for the mobile marketing billboard effect they offered.

He was the first service contractor to do a flat rate. He was the first contractor to give his technicians handheld computers (loaded with the Blau price book). He started the practice of valve tags. He developed a simple, efficient, and effective inventory control system. He created his own truck shelving system that maximizes inventory and simplifies inventory control.

Frank has always been an innovator and a pioneer. He's got the arrows in his back to prove it. But like the lead sled dog, Frank's always had the better view.

Maybe Frank's greatest innovation is also his simplest. He came to the revelation that plumbers, operating at the top of their game, should be rewarded for their efforts. Not only should the owners be rewarded, Frank concluded, but also the plumbers and technicians who helped them earn their wealth.

Frank paid his people well, gave them and their families health insurance, and created profit sharing and fully funded retirement plans. If a plumber was to give Frank twenty to twenty-five years of service, Frank wanted him to be able to retire in comfort. His motives come from the heart. Frank chokes up when he talks about the wealth his employees managed to accumulate through his company.

So Much to Give

If this was the story, it would be a good one. But this is merely the start of Frank Blau's story. Other plumbing contractors heard about the things going on at Blau Plumbing, and they sought Frank out to learn more. Frank welcomed them and selflessly taught them.

The demand and need were so great that Frank went on the road. He taught pricing seminars from coast to coast. He wrote a very popular and widely read column in *Plumbing & Mechanical* (that Service Roundtable plumbing czar Randall Hilton now writes). When he couldn't convince his trade association to focus on the service business, Frank was instrumental in the foundation of Contractors 2000 (now Nexstar), one of the first contractor alliances.

Frank's message was first that contractors "should" earn a decent living, "should" be able to take care of their people, and "could." You might say that Frank became the psychotherapist for an industry.

Once he convinced someone he or she deserved more, Frank taught that person how. He taught him or her how to allocate overhead and price for profits. As his books are titled, Frank taught the "Business of Contracting" to thousands. He taught thousands how to make a living.

Few people have given as much to others as Frank. The lost would read his column and call him. He took these calls from strangers he had never met, gave them a seminar on the phone, told them to "take the medicine," and pointed the way to the Promised Land of profitability.

When the Service Roundtable first announced the creation of the Servant Leader Award, it took all of thirty seconds for the first of our members to nominate Frank (first but not the last). Frank was presented with the award last week. The inscription on the statue reads, "The truest, most noble form of leadership is that of 'servant leadership.' The Servant Leader leads by example, not command. The Servant Leader is compelled to help others, to serve. The Servant Leader Award recognizes individuals who have selflessly devoted a lifetime to serving others in their field. They are servants first, who have become notable leaders through their service to their fellows, enriching us all."

Frank Blau has led by example his entire life. He has served his customers, his employees, and his industry. Through his service he became the most renowned leader in the field of plumbing.

Today, Frank has retired as a wealthy man. He purchased a large tract of land in west central Wisconsin, built a hunting cabin, and is practicing quality deer management with the same enthusiasm, vigor, and excellence he applied to his business and profession.

Frank has been a mentor to many. As a successful businessperson, he's been a role model. Yet, his greatest professional role is that of servant leader. We should all aspire to positively touch as many lives as Frank Blau. We should all aspire to become servant leaders like Frank Blau.

Here's to you, Frank!

CHAPTER 29

Future Generations

To HAVE BEEN an instrument of change—that was what Frank's mother asked of him when he was a young man. Frank said,

> To improve the lives of hundreds of contractors and thousands of their employees throughout the industry—nothing has been more gratifying in my professional life.
>
> I'm referring to the contractors from coast to coast who have "taken the medicine" and revamped their business practices to get the selling prices they need to succeed in business and leave a legacy to their families, employees, and communities at large.
>
> Ensuring the next generation will have it better than the last—this, my friends, is our one true purpose.

If you learn anything in this world that is valuable, you must share it with your fellow man before you die because each generation must have it better than the previous generation.

— Marie Blau

ADVICE FOR THE NEXT GENERATION, BY FRANK BLAU

1. Find successful people and hang out with them.
2. Find quality time to read and comprehend. No interruptions. Take time to think and understand. You may read something, like I did, that changes your life. You don't have time to read? Read in the middle of the night.

3. Find a mentor. Someone who will kick your ass. But you have to find someone who is really rich. There are imposters. Ask to see their balance sheet and their P&L. Make them prove their success to you.

4. Plan so you can afford to ease into retirement. Too many contractors keep working long beyond the time they should be expected to. It doesn't have to be that way.

5. I've missed out on many events in the lives of children and grandchildren because I spent so much time on the road traveling and presenting my seminars. Don't let these things pass you by. Make time to attend your kids' ball games, school plays, and whatever other activities they may participate in. Once they grow up, it's too late to make up for lost time.

EPILOGUE

———— ❧ ————

Ellen's Story

I ALMOST TANKED our family business. I assumed I knew enough about business to run a little plumbing company. After all, I had spent about $100,000 of my parents' money on my college degree in business administration. I graduated at the top of my class. I had oodles of business and work experience.

Boy, was I wrong.

I got involved in my husband Hotrod's company after his partner died unexpectedly. Once we got over the initial shock and grief, I turned to Hotrod and said, "I'll quit my job and come work for you. You turn wrenches. I'll count the money. We'll get rich."

The problem was, though it seemed like lots of money was moving through the company, at the end of the month there was never any money left. It was humbling.

Thankfully, I found Frank. Frank J. Blau Jr. wrote a column in *Plumbing & Mechanical* magazine. In this particular issue, his article was on how much a contractor should charge.

I'm a smart chick. I followed the math. Frank suggested—get this— that you should add up all your costs of doing business and then charge more than that. Mind blowing, right? But here's the thing. I thought you had to charge what the market would bear. I learned in college that you had to abide by the "going rate" for goods and service.

So I wrote Frank a letter on cheap stationery—because that's all I could afford. I opened with a short paragraph asking for help. Then I spent two pages telling him that he was wrong. I laid out all the reasons why what he suggested in his article would never work.

I cringe now, thinking about it. (You can check out the letter in *The Business of Contracting* by Frank Blau.)

A few days later, at seven o'clock in the morning, the phone rang.

I was in my corporate attire (bathrobe) with baby Max on my hip, trying to get Hotrod and the other plumbers out the door. I picked up the phone. "Hello."

A gruff voice on the other end of the line said, "Hello? Is this a business? Residence? What?"

Like I needed this at seven o'clock. I responded impatiently, "It's both. May I help you?"

The next thing I heard was, "Honey, you have your head so far up your (um, you get the idea), you will never see the light of day. This is Frank Blau. I just read your letter. I get a lot of stupid letters. This one takes the cake. You think you know so much. Then why are you so broke? You don't want help. You just want to prove how right you are. You asked for help. I'm giving it. Shut the business down."

Well. Frank Blau. The columnist from the magazine. And I couldn't believe how he was talking to me. Rattled, I stumbled through his "margin-versus-markup quiz." (I failed.) I got off the phone as fast as I could. Then I got mad. *How dare he!*

When Hotrod came home from work, I told him about the phone call. I fumed, "He told me where my head was. He said we should just close the doors. He made me cry!"

Hotrod responded, "I think you should call him back. We don't know what we are doing, and we are in debt up to our eyeballs."

Sigh. He was right. My anger was replaced with humility and then abject fear. We were in big trouble, and I needed help.

The next day I called Frank back. I apologized and asked him to mentor me. Frank took me under his wing and taught me how to keep score in business. He taught me how to read and use financial reports. He sent his own financials over via fax. Remember that messy thermal fax paper? Scrolls of it would pour forth from our fax machine so Frank could teach me my asset from my elbow. He taught me how to make money. He held me accountable and told me, "Your ass is grass, and I'm the lawn mower."

We turned our company around. We paid off our loans. We doubled sales and tripled the amount of money we took out of the company. Very cool.

Hotrod and I went middle-aged crazy. We sold the company to our employees (a friendly coup d'état!) and bought a gentleman's farm in the country. Picture *Green Acres.*

It was at this point that I realized I wanted to share what I'd learned. After all, if a smart, highly educated person like me didn't know how to read a balance sheet, I figured business illiteracy must be rampant. I was right. So I am proud to add to Frank's legacy by helping others learn business basics, like I did once upon a time.

That was thirty-five years ago. Since then, Frank has been a constant mentor and amazing friend. Not just to me. Thousands of people have benefited from his wisdom and tough love. Frank J. Blau Jr. has changed me and the entire contracting industry for the better. Not only is he a master of the financial aspects of business; he's also a master marketer, business manager, and philosopher, all rolled up into one.

In fact, everything Frank takes on he masters. Just get him started on marketing and selling prices and wildlife preservation and the best recipe for chili. He is truly a renaissance man.

We are all the richer—financially and personally—for the life and legacy of Frank J. Blau Jr.

Ellen Rohr

President, http://www.EllenRohr.com

P.S. Let us know how Frank has impacted your life. Join the conversation at www.nexstarnetwork.com/meetfrankblau. Tell us your Frank story or anecdote, or upload a picture. We look forward to hearing from you.

Appendix

Solution to the Hypothetical Selling Price Exercise

Material   15% Overhead
Labor Direct Cost   10% Net Profit

If Materials and Labor Direct Cost represents 75% of the total selling price, to get to the proper selling price, you need to divide the Direct Cost by 75%. $1,000/75% = $1,333.33

Check your work:

15% Overhead Dollars	$200.00
10% Net Profit Dollars	$133.00
Total Overhead and Net Profit Dollars	$333.00

Subtract the overhead and net profit dollars from selling price. The correct answer should equal material and labor cost, and it does: $1,333–$333 = $1,000

Timeline

---∞---

Chronology of Professional Achievements and Accomplishments

1929

- Frank J Blau Jr. is born to Polish immigrants Frank J Blau and the former Marie Krason on February 23 in Milwaukee. He has three siblings: Jimmy, Margie, and Eddie.

1939

- The young entrepreneur shines shoes and does errands so he can have something.

1945

- He defies his father to attend private high school. He pays his own tuition by working at a filling station.

1946

- He saves the life of his father and friend by swimming to shore after boat capsizes.
- He meets Irene Shimmels in art class during his freshman year.

1947

- He is a football all-star.

1947

- He goes to college; he is a mortuary science major; he goes to dental school, studying liberal arts. It's not for him.

- He goes to work at an auto plant, Seimans. He learns to weld but finds factory work stultifying. He hangs in there.

1950
- Frank and Irene marry.
- He buys his first home.

1951
- His daughter Joanie is born.

1952
- His son Jimmy is born.

1954
- His son Frank E. is born.

1955
- His fourth child, Tommy, is born.
- He becomes a journeyman plumber.
- He leaves plumbing to join his brothers in Butler Auto Body.

1958
- He leaves Butler Auto Body and returns to the plumbing trade as a superintendent/foreman for John Debelak.
- His son Bobby is born.

1959
- He drives into a train on the way to Milwaukee and lives to tell the tale.

1960
- He starts Blau Plumbing with $600 in working capital.
- His sixth child, John, is born.

- He earns his master plumber degree.
- He joins MPHCC.

1961

- He attends the Fundamentals of Selling Course, PHCIB.
- His daughter Janet is born.

1962

- He reads "markup and margin" article in *Domestic Engineering* magazine, and it changes everything.

1963

- His brother Eddie joins the business.
- He and John Debelak take up golf.
- He establishes his first showroom.
- His daughter Mary is born.

1964

- He becomes president of the Germantown School Board.

1966

- Steven Francis Blau is born. He dies at age eight months in 1967.

1968

- His son William Steven is born.

1973

- He shifts his business focus from new construction to service.

1974

- He survives another close call on a boat, this time in the Gulf of Mexico—with sharks.

1978

- His peers vote him in as Wisconsin Contractor of the Year.

1981–1982
- He serves as president of the MPCA.

1985

- He meets the publisher of *Plumbing & Mechanical* magazine at National Kitchen & Bath show.

1987

- He begins writing columns for *PM.*

1988

- He discovers the concept of flat rate after seeing *Ward's Crash Book* at brother's auto dealership.

1989

- He publishes "How Much Should a Contractor Charge?" in *PM* magazine.
- He serves as an expert witness for a Phoenix contractor, whose partner sued him under the RICOH Act.
- He runs for NAPHCC president and loses.
- He decides to start his own organization with George Brazil.

1992

- He founds Contractors 2000 with George Brazil and sixteen others.
- He travels the country, teaching the "Business of Contracting" and consulting.

2003

- He purchases 135 acres in northern Wisconsin. He becomes a farmer and deer management expert.
- He retires from writing for *PM* magazine after sixteen years.

2004

- He officially retires and transfers ownership of Blau Plumbing to his sons Jimmy and Bobby.
- He is awarded lifetime membership in Nexstar.

2005

- He receives the Servant Leader Award from Service Roundtable.
- Nexstar Legacy Foundation is established. He is awarded lifetime membership in the Legacy Foundation.

2009

- *PM* names him as "Most Influential Contractor of the Past 25 Years" in the March 2009 issue of *PM* magazine.

2012

- He is honored at Nexstar's twenty-year anniversary.

2014

- The Frank J. Blau Jr. Training Center is dedicated.

2015

- *Soaring with Eagles: The Life and Legacy of Frank J. Blau Jr.* is published, and www.nexstarnetwork.com/meetfrankblau, a tribute website, is launched.

About the Authors

ELLEN ROHR IS a plumber's wife, business makeover expert, and Frank Blau devotee. She shares her Business Uncomplicated—Life Unleashed philosophy, books, tools, and classes at http://www.ellenrohr.com.

"Thanks to Frank for sharing his story with us! And thanks to Helena for moving it into book reality. You rock, sister!" —Ellen

Helena Bouchez is a business storyteller and book shepherd, specializing in the development of evergreen business books and inspiring executive biographies. Find out more at http://www.executivewords.com.

"Partnering with Ellen to tell Frank's story changed my life. Thanks to both Frank Blau Jr. and Peter Shankman for bringing us together. Rock on, El!" —Helena

Visit www.nexstarnetwork.com/meetfrankblau and add your stories and pictures to Frank's legacy.

Made in the USA
Columbia, SC
23 December 2018